Autodesk Inventor 2019 For Beginners Part 1 (Part Modeling)

Tutorial Books

Table of Contents

Introduction 11

Topics covered in this Book...11

Chapter 1: Getting Started with Autodesk Inventor 2019 13

Introduction to Autodesk Inventor 2019 13

Starting Autodesk Inventor 2019...15

File Types..16

User Interface 16

Environments in Autodesk Inventor 17

Part environment...17

Assembly environment 17

Drawing environment 18

Sheet Metal environment 18

File Menu..18

Quick Access Toolbar 19

Graphics Window 19

Status Bar...20

Quick View Cube 21

Dialogs 21

Changing the display of the Ribbon 21

Marking Menus 23

Shortcut Menus 23

Starting a new document...23

The Create New dialog..24

Application Options dialog 24

Changing the Color Scheme 25

Autodesk Inventor Help 26

Questions..26

Chapter 2: Sketch techniques 29

Sketching in the Sketch environment 29

Sketch Commands..29

The Line command 30

Creating Arcs..30

Creating Circles 33

Creating Rectangles 33

Creating Slots..35

The Polygon command..37

The Ellipse command..39

The Dimension command...39

Linear Dimensions...40

Angular Dimensions..41

Adding Dimensions to an Arc...41

Over-constrained Sketch..42

Constraints..43

Coincident Constraint...43

Horizontal Constraint...44

Vertical Constraint..44

Concentric Constraint...45

Equal...45

Collinear Constraint..46

Tangent...46

Parallel Constraint..46

Perpendicular Constraint...47

Symmetric..47

Constraint Settings..48

The Inference tab...48

Show/Hide All Constraints...49

Adding Dimensions and Constraints Automatically..49

The Construction Command...50

The Centerline Command..50

The Fillet command..51

The Chamfer command...52

The Extend command..53

The Trim command..53

The Offset command..53

The Move command...54

The Copy command...54

The Rotate command...54

The Scale command..55

The Stretch command..55

Circular Sketch Pattern 56

Rectangular Sketch Pattern 57

The Mirror command 57

Creating Splines 58

TUTORIAL 1 (Millimeters) 59

    Starting a Sketch 60

    Adding Constraints 61

    Adding Dimensions 62

    Finishing the Sketch and Saving it 66

TUTORIAL 2 (Inches) 66

    Starting a Sketch 67

TUTORIAL 3 (Millimeters) 72

    Starting a Sketch 73

Questions 79

    Exercise 1 80

    Exercise 2 80

    Exercise 3 80

Chapter 3: Extrude and Revolve Features 81

Extruded Features 81

Revolved Features 82

Project Geometry 82

Planes 83

    Offset from Plane 83

    Parallel to Plane through Point 84

    Midplane between Two Planes 84

    Midplane of Torus 85

    Angle to Plane around Edge 86

    Three Points 86

    Two Coplanar Edges 86

    Tangent to Surface through Edge 87

    Tangent to Surface through Point 88

    Tangent to Surface and Parallel to Plane 88

    Normal to Axis through Point 89

    Normal to Curve at a Point 89

UCS 90

Additional options of the Extrude command..91

    Operation...91

    New Solid...92

    Extents 92

    Match Shape..95

    Adding Taper to the Extruded Feature...95

View Modification commands...97

TUTORIAL 1 (Millimeters)...99

    Creating the Base Feature 99

    Creating the Extrude Cut throughout the Part model 101

    Creating the Extruded Cut up to the surface next to the sketch plane 103

    Extruding the sketch up to a Surface...106

TUTORIAL 2 (Inches) 108

    Creating the Revolved Solid Feature..108

    Creating the Revolved Cut..110

    Adding a Revolved Feature to the model..111

    Questions...113

Chapter 4: Placed Features **117**

Hole 117

    Simple Hole...118

    Counterbored Hole 121

    Countersink Hole 122

    Tapped Hole 122

    Taper Tapped Hole 123

Thread 123

Fillet...124

    Smooth Fillet...125

    Inverted Fillet..125

    Variable Radius Fillet 127

    Corner Setback..128

    Face Fillet..129

Full Round Fillet..129

Chamfer 129

    Distance and Angle chamfer...130

    Two Distances chamfer...130

The Face Draft command 130

Shell 132

TUTORIAL 1 (Millimeters) 133

Chapter 5: Patterned Geometry **145**

Mirror 146

Mirror Solids 147

Rectangular Pattern 148

Using the Compute options 149

Creating a Pattern Along a Path 150

Patterning the entire geometry 151

Suppressing Occurrences 151

Circular Pattern 151

Sketch Driven Pattern 153

TUTORIAL 1 (Millimeters) 154

Questions 160

Exercises 161

Exercise 1 (Millimetres) 161

Chapter 6: Sweep Features **163**

Path sweeps 164

Profile Orientation 167

Taper 167

Twist 167

Path and Guide Rail Sweeps 168

Path and Guide Surface Sweeps 169

Swept Cutout 170

Coil 171

Helical Cutout 175

Examples 175

Example 1 (Inches) 175

Questions 181

Exercises 181

Exercise1 181

Chapter 7: Loft Features **183**

Loft 183

Loft sections 183

Conditions 184

Rails 186

Closed Loop 187

Center Line Loft 188

Area Loft 188

Loft Cutout 190

Examples 190

Example 1 (Millimetres) 190

Questions 194

Exercises 195

Exercise 1 195

Chapter 8: Additional Features and Multibody Parts..**197**

Rib 197

Applying Draft to the Rib Feature 198

Adding a Boss to the Rib feature 199

Bend Part 200

Multi-body Parts 200

Creating Multibodies 200

The Split command 201

Join 203

Intersect 204

Cut 204

Emboss 204

Decal 206

Example 1 (Inches) 206

Example 1 (Millimetres) 211

Questions 217

Exercises 218

Exercise 1 218

Exercise 2 219

Exercise 3 (Inches) 220

Chapter 9: Modifying Parts **223**

Edit Sketches 223

Edit Feature 224

Suppress Features 224

Resume Suppressed Features 224

Examples...225

    Example 1 (Inches) 225

    Example 2 (Millimetres) 228

Questions..230

Exercises...231

    Exercise 1 231

Introduction

Welcome to *Autodesk Inventor 2019 For Beginners* book. This book is written to assist students, designers, and engineering professionals in designing 3D models. It covers the important features and functionalities of Autodesk Inventor using relevant examples and exercises.

This book is written for new users, who can use it as a self-study resource to learn Autodesk Inventor. In addition, experienced users can also use it as a reference. The focus of this book is part modeling.

Topics covered in this Book

- Chapter 1, "Getting Started with Autodesk Inventor 2019", gives an introduction to Autodesk Inventor. The user interface and terminology are discussed in this chapter.

- Chapter 2, "Sketch Techniques", explores the sketching commands in Autodesk Inventor. You will learn to create parametric sketches.

- Chapter 3, "Extrude and Revolve features", teaches you to create basic 3D geometry using the Extrude and Revolve commands.

- Chapter 4, "Placed Features", covers the features which can be created without using sketches.

- Chapter 5, "Patterned Geometry", explores the commands to create patterned and mirrored geometry.

- Chapter 6, "Sweep Features", covers the commands to create swept and helical features.

- Chapter 7, "Loft Features", covers the Loft command and its core features.

- Chapter 8, "Additional Features and Multibody Parts", covers additional commands to create complex geometry. In addition, the multibody parts are also covered.

- Chapter 9, "Modifying Parts", explores the commands and techniques to modify the part geometry.

Chapter 1: Getting Started with Autodesk Inventor 2019

Introduction to Autodesk Inventor 2019

Autodesk Inventor is a parametric and feature-based system that allows you to create 3D parts, assemblies, and 2D drawings. The design process in Autodesk Inventor is shown below.

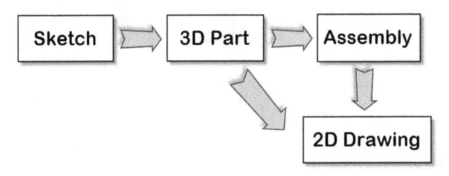

In Inventor, everything is controlled by parameters, dimensions, or constraints. For example, if you want to change the position of the hole shown in figure, you need to change the dimension or relation that controls its position.

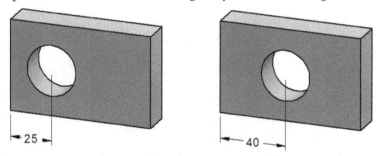

The parameters and constraints that you set up allow you to have control over the design intent. The design intent describes the way your 3D model will behave when you apply dimensions and constraints to it. For example, if you want to position the hole at the center of the block, one way is to add dimensions between the hole and the adjacent edges. However, when you change the size of the block, the hole will not be at the center.

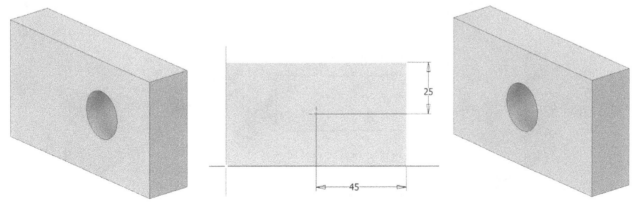

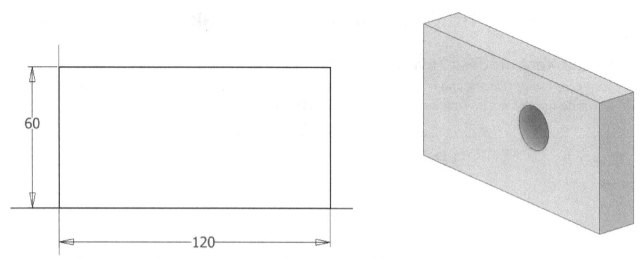

You can make the hole to be at the center, even if the size of the block changes. To do this, click on the hole feature and select **Edit Sketch**. Next, delete the dimensions and create a diagonal construction line. Apply the Coincident constraint between the hole point and the midpoint of the diagonal construction line. Next, click **Finish Sketch** on the ribbon.

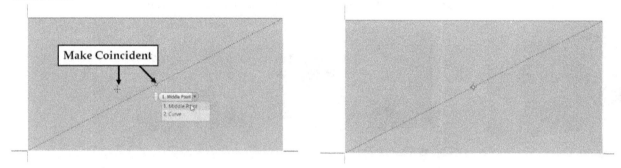

Now, even if you change the size of the block, the hole will always remain at the center.

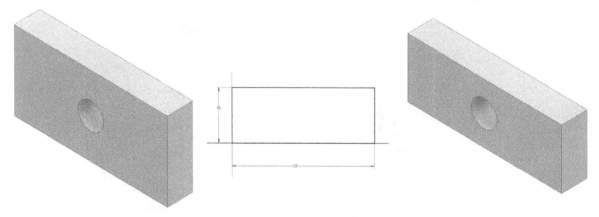

The other big advantage of Autodesk Inventor is the associativity between parts, assemblies and drawings. When you make changes to the design of a part, the changes will take place in any assembly that it's a part of. In addition, the 2D drawing will update automatically.

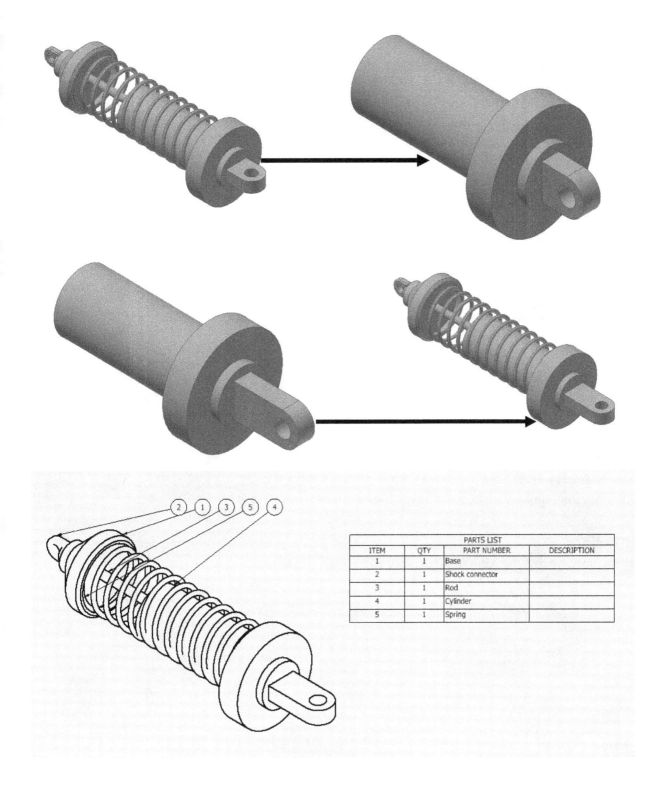

PARTS LIST			
ITEM	QTY	PART NUMBER	DESCRIPTION
1	1	Base	
2	1	Shock connector	
3	1	Rod	
4	1	Cylinder	
5	1	Spring	

Starting Autodesk Inventor 2019

To start **Autodesk Inventor 2019**, click the **Autodesk Inventor 2019** icon on your computer screen. To start a new part or assembly or drawing file, then click **New** option button under **Launch** panel on the **Get Started** Tab. Click **Metric** under the **Templates** folder on the **Create New File** dialog to start a new part document. Then, click **Standard(mm). ipt** under **Part – Create 2D and 3D objects**, and then click the **Create** button.

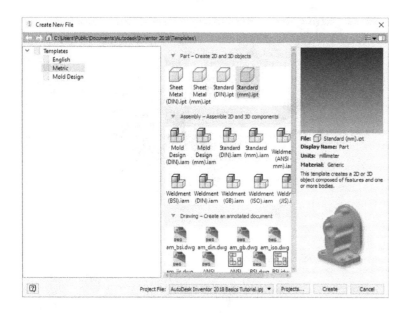

File Types

Various file types that can be created in Autodesk Inventor are given below.

- **Part (.ipt)**
- **Assembly (.iam)**
- **Drawing (.dwg)**
- **Sheet Metal (.ipt)**
- **Presentation (.ipn)**

User Interface

The following image shows the **Autodesk Inventor** application window.

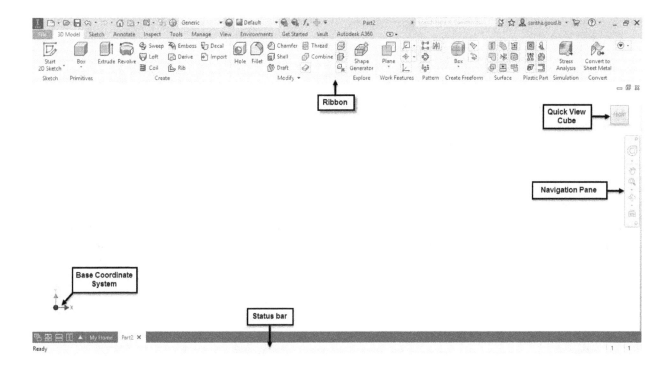

Environments in Autodesk Inventor

There are five main environments available in Autodesk Inventor: **Part**, **Assembly**, **Drawing**, **Presentation**, and **Sheet Metal**. In addition, there are some additional environments to create exploded views, renderings, simulations, and so on.

Part environment

This environment has all the commands to create a 3D part model. It has a ribbon located at the top of the screen. The ribbon is arranged in a hierarchy of tabs, panels, and commands. Panels such as **Sketch**, **Create**, and **Modify** consists of commands, which are grouped based on their usage. Panels in turn are grouped into various tabs. For example, the panels such as **Sketch**, **Create**, and **Modify** are located in the **3D Model** tab.

Assembly environment

This environment is used to create assemblies. The **Assemble** tab of the Ribbon has various commands, which will allow you to assemble and modify the components.

The **3D Model** tab in the Assembly environment has commands, which will help you to create holes, fillets and other features at the assembly level.

The **Inspect** tab helps you to inspect the assembly geometry.

The **Tools** tab has some advanced commands, which will help you to access application options, document settings, and appearance options. In addition to that, you can customize the environment, automate processes, and add external apps.

Drawing environment

This environment has all the commands to generate 2D drawings of parts and assemblies.

Sheet Metal environment

This environment has commands to create sheet metal parts.

The other components of the user interface are discussed next.

File Menu

The **File Menu** appears when you click on the **File** tab located at the top left corner of the window. The **File Menu** consists of a list of self-explanatory menus. You can see a list of recently opened documents under **Recent Documents** menu located on the right side.

Quick Access Toolbar

This is located at the top left corner of the window. It consists of commonly used commands such as **New, Save, Open,** and so on. You can add more commands to the **Quick Access Toolbar** by clicking on the down-arrow next to the **Design doctor** icon, and then selecting them from the pop-up menu.

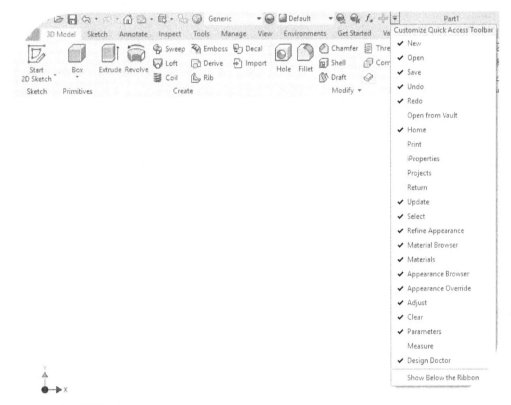

Graphics Window

Graphics window is the blank space located below the ribbon. You can draw sketches and create 3D geometry in the Graphics window. The left corner of the graphics window has a **Model window**. Using the **Model window**, you can access the features of the 3D model.

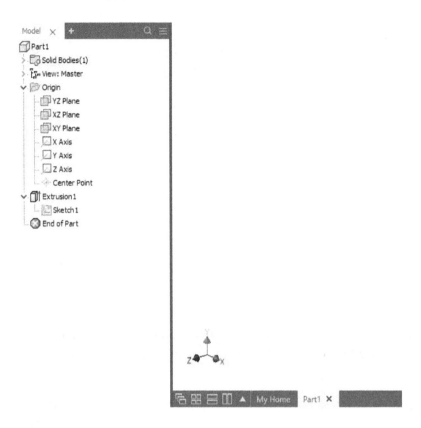

Status Bar

Status Bar is located at the bottom of the Autodesk Inventor window. It is useful when you activate a command. It displays various prompts while working with any command. These prompts are series of steps needed to create a feature successfully.

For Help, press F1

The **Search Help & Commands** bar is used to search for any command available in Autodesk Inventor 2019. It is located at the top right side of the title bar. You can type any keyword in the **Search Help & Commands** bar and find a list of commands related to it.

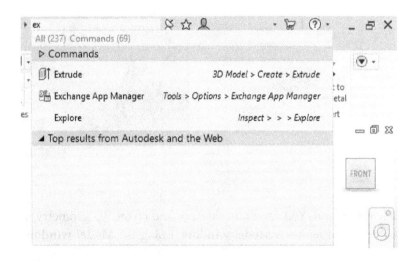

View Cube

It is located at the top right corner of the graphics window and is used to set the view orientation of the model.

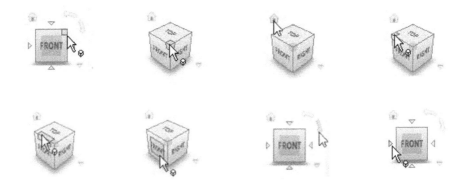

Dialogs

Dialogs are part of Autodesk Inventor user interface. Using a dialog, you can easily specify many settings and options. Various components of a dialog are shown below.

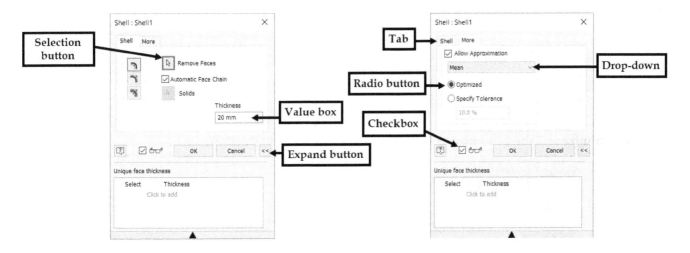

Changing the display of the Ribbon

You can add or remove commands from the ribbon by clicking the right mouse button on it, and then selecting **Customize User Commands**. On the **Customize** dialog, click on the commands in the list box located at the left side, and then click **Add** ; the command is added to the ribbon. If you want to remove the command from the ribbon, then select it from the list box located at the right side. Next, click the **Remove** button. After making the required changes, click **OK** to save the changes.

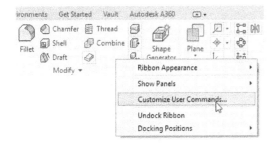

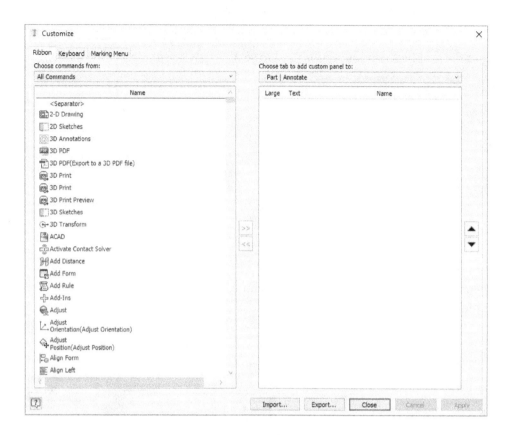

You can minimize the ribbon by clicking on the **Minimize to Panel Buttons** down arrow. It lists three different options: **Minimize to Tabs, Minimize to Panel Titles** and **Minimize to Panel Buttons**.

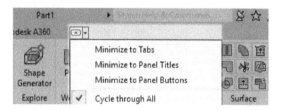

Select the **Minimize to Tabs** option to display only tabs.

Select the **Minimize to Panel Titles** option to display both tabs and panel titles.

Select the **Minimize to Panel Buttons** option to display both tabs and panels.

Marking Menus

Marking Menus provide you with another way of activating commands. You can display Marking Menus by clicking the right mouse button. A Marking Menu has various commands arranged in a radial manner. You can add or remove commands to the Marking Menu by using the **Customize** dialog.

Shortcut Menus

Shortcut Menus are displayed when you right-click in the graphics window. Autodesk Inventor provides various shortcut menus in order to help you access some options very easily and quickly. The options in shortcut menus vary based on the environment.

Starting a new document

You can start a new document directly from the **My Home** screen or by using the **Create New** dialog. On the **My Home** screen, click on the required option to start a part, assembly, drawing, or a presentation document.

The Create New dialog

To start a new document using the **Create New** dialog, click the **New** button on anyone of the following:

- **Quick Access Toolbar**
- **File Menu**
- **Launch** panel of the **Get Started** ribbon tab

The **Create New File** dialog appears when you click the **New** button. In this dialog, select the required standard from the **Templates** section. The templates related to the selected standard will appear. Select the .iam, .dwg, .ipt, or .ipn templates to start an assembly, drawing, part, or presentation file, respectively.

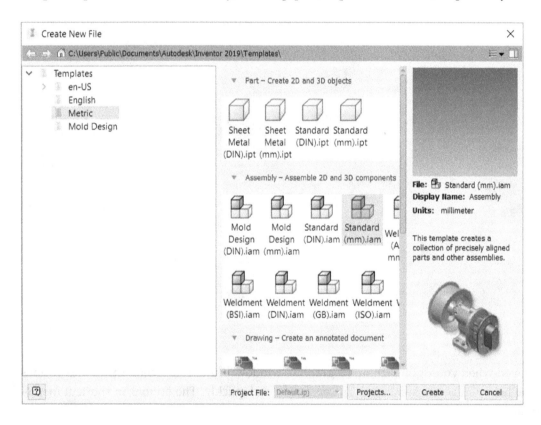

Application Options dialog

You can use the **Application Options** dialog to customize Autodesk Inventor as per your requirement. On the **File Menu**, click the **Options** button to open the **Application Options** dialog. On this dialog, you can set options on each of the tabs.

Changing the Color Scheme

The **Colors** tab of the **Application Options** dialog helps you to change the background color, reflection environment, and Color Theme. On the ribbon, click **Tools > Options > Application Options** to open this dialog. On this dialog, click the **Colors** tab and set the **Color scheme** to **Presentation**. Next, select **Background > 1 Color**, and then click **OK**; the background color changes to white.

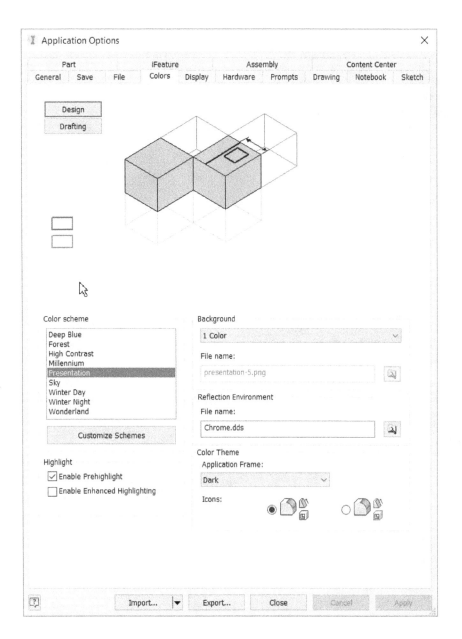

Autodesk Inventor Help

Autodesk Inventor offers you with the help system that goes beyond basic command definition. You can access Autodesk Inventor help by using any of the following methods:

- Press the **F1** key.

- Click on the **Autodesk Inventor Help** ⌐②⌐ option on the right-side of the window.

Questions

1. Explain how to customize the Ribbon.

2. What is design intent?

3. Give one example of where you would establish a relationship between a part's features.

4. Explain the term 'associativity' in Autodesk Inventor.

5. List any two procedures to access Autodesk Inventor Help.

6. How to change the background color of the graphics window?

7. How to activate the Marking Menu?

8. How is Autodesk Inventor a parametric modeling application?

Chapter 2: Sketch techniques

This chapter covers the methods and commands to create sketches in the part environment. The commands and methods are discussed in context to part environment. In Inventor, you create a rough sketch, and then apply dimensions and constraints that define its shape and size. The dimensions define the length, size, and angle of a sketch element, whereas constraints define the relations between sketch elements.

In this chapter, you will:

- Create sketches in the Sketch Environment
- Use constraints and dimensions to control the shape and size of a sketch
- Learn sketching commands
- Learn commands and options that help you to create sketches easily

Sketching in the Sketch environment

Autodesk Inventor provides you a separate environment to create sketches. It is called the Sketch environment. To activate this environment, click **3D Model > Sketch > Start 2D Sketch** on the ribbon. Next, click on any of the Planes located at the center of the graphics window. The **Sketch** tab appears on the ribbon. On this tab, you can find different sketch commands. You can use these commands and start drawing the sketch on the selected plane. After creating the sketch, click **Sketch > Exit > Finish Sketch** on the ribbon to finish the sketch.

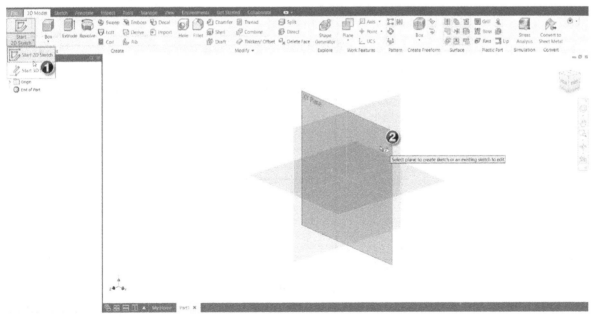

Sketch Commands

Autodesk Inventor provides you with a set of commands to create sketches. These commands are located on the **Create** panel of the **Sketch** ribbon.

The Line command

This is the most commonly used command while creating a sketch. To activate this command, click **Sketch > Create > Line** on the ribbon. As you move the pointer in the graphics window, you will notice that a box is attached to it. It displays the X and Y coordinates of the pointer. To create a line, click in the graphics window, move the pointer and click again. After clicking for the second time, you can see that an end point is added and another line segment is started. This is a convenient way to create a chain of lines. Continue to click to add more line segments. You can right-click in the graphics window and click **Restart**, if you want to end the chain. Now, start creating a separate line chain. Right click and select **OK** or press **Esc** to deactivate the **Line** command.

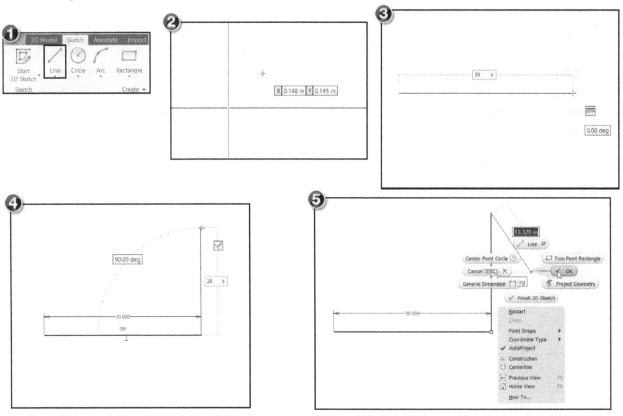

Tip: To create a horizontal line, specify the start point of the line and move the pointer horizontally; the Horizontal constraint glyph appears next to the pointer. Click to create a horizontal line. In addition, the Horizontal constraint is applied to the line. You will learn about constraints later in this chapter. Likewise, you can create a vertical line by moving the pointer vertically and clicking.

Creating Arcs

Autodesk Inventor allows you to create an arc using three commands: **Arc by Three Point** , **Arc by Tangent** and **Arc by Center Point.**

The Arc Three Point command

This command creates an arc by defining its start, end and radius. Activate the **Arc Three Point** command, by clicking **Sketch** tab > **Create** panel > **Arc** drop-down > **Arc Three Point** on the ribbon. In the graphics window, click to define the start point of the arc. Next, move the pointer and click again to define the end point of the arc. After defining the start and end of the arc, you need to define the size and position of the arc. To do this, move the pointer and click to define the radius and position of the arc.

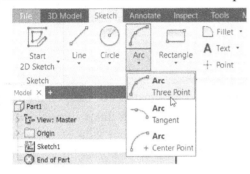
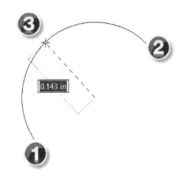

The Arc Tangent Command

This command creates an arc tangent to another entity. To activate this command, click **Sketch** > **Create** > **Arc** drop-down > **Arc Tangent** on the ribbon. Click on the endpoint of the entity to start the arc. The arc is tangent to the starting entity. Move the pointer and click to define the radius and position of the arc.

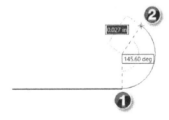

Autodesk Inventor allows you to create an arc tangent to the line without activating the **Tangent Arc** command. To do this, activate the **Line** command and create a line. Next, move the pointer away, and then take it back to the end point of the line. Now, press and hold the left mouse button and drag the pointer in-line with the existing line. Next, drag the pointer to either side of the existing line to specify the size and direction of the arc. After dragging up to the required distance, release the left mouse button to specify the end point of the arc.

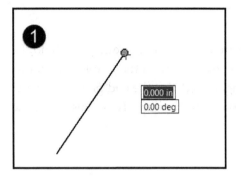 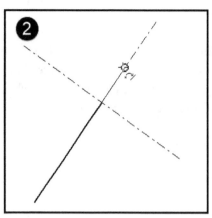 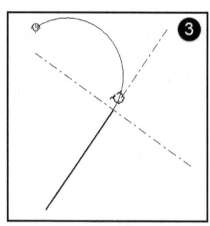

If you want to create a normal arc using the **Line** command, then first create a line. Next, move the pointer away from the endpoint, and then move it back. Press and hold the left mouse button and drag the pointer along the dotted line displayed perpendicular to the existing line. Next, drag the pointer on either side of the dotted perpendicular line to specify the size and direction of the normal arc. After dragging up to the required distance, release the left mouse button to define the endpoint of the arc.

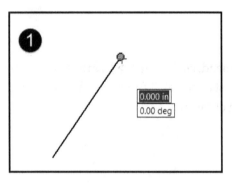 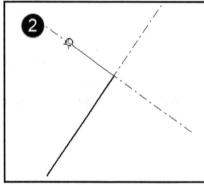 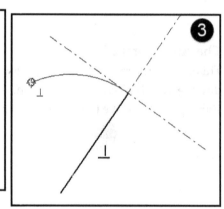

The Center Point Arc command

This command creates an arc by defining its center, start and end. Activate the **Center Point Arc** command, by clicking **Sketch > Create > Arc** drop-down **> Arc Center Point** on the ribbon. Click to define the center point. Next, move the pointer and you will notice that a dotted line appears between center and the pointer. This line is the radius of the arc. Now, click to define the start point of the arc and move the pointer; you will notice that an arc is drawn from the start point. Once the arc appears the way you want, click to define its end point.

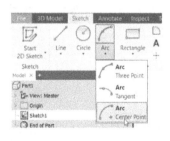  

Creating Circles

Inventor allows you to create a circle using two commands: **Center Point Circle** and **Tangent Circle**.

Center Point Circle

This is the most common way to draw a circle. Activate the **Center Point Circle** command, by clicking **Sketch > Create > Circle** drop-down > **Circle Center Point** on the ribbon. Click to define the center point of the circle. Drag the pointer, and then click again to define the diameter of the circle.

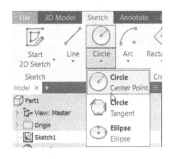 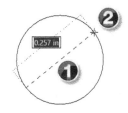 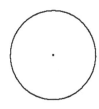

Tangent Circle

This command creates a circle tangent to three lines. Activate this command by clicking **Sketch > Create > Circle** drop-down > **Circle Tangent** on the ribbon. Select three lines from the graphics window; a circle is created tangent to the selected lines.

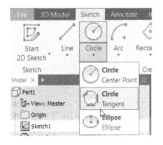 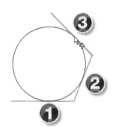 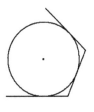

Creating Rectangles

Inventor allows you to create a rectangle using four different commands: **Two Point Rectangle, Three Point Rectangle, Two Point Center Rectangle**, and **Three Point Center Rectangle**.

Two Point Rectangle

This command creates a rectangle by defining its diagonal corners. Activate the **Two Point Rectangle** command (On the ribbon, click **Sketch > Create > Rectangle** drop-down > **Rectangle Two Point**). In the graphics window, click to define the first corner of the rectangle. Move the pointer and click to define the second corner. You can also type-in values in the boxes attached to the pointer.

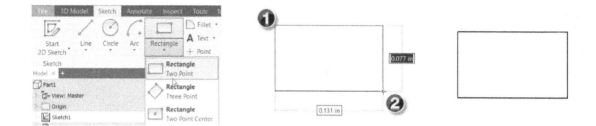

Three Point Rectangle

This command creates an inclined rectangle. Activate the **Three Point Rectangle** command (On the ribbon, click **Sketch > Create > Rectangle** drop-down > **Rectangle Three Point**). Specify the first two points to define the width and inclination angle of the rectangle. You can also enter width and inclination angle values in the value boxes displayed in the graphics window. Next, specify the third point to define the height of the rectangle.

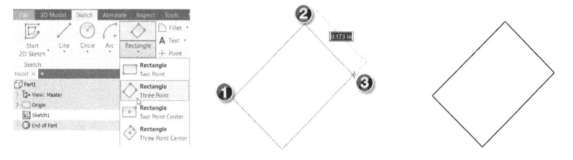

Two Point Center Rectangle

This command creates a rectangle using two points: center and corner points. Activate the **Rectangle Two Point Center** command (On the ribbon, click **Sketch > Create > Rectangle** drop-down > **Rectangle Two Point Center**). In the graphics window, click to define the first point as a center of the rectangle. Next, specify the corner point to define the width and height of the rectangle. You can also type-in the values in the value boxes displayed in the graphics window.

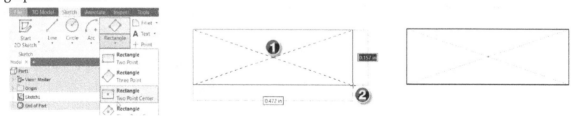

Three Point Center Rectangle

This command creates a rectangle using three points: center, midpoint of the first side, and corner point. Activate the **Three Point Center Rectangle** command (On the ribbon, click **Sketch > Create > Rectangle** drop-down > **Rectangle Three Point Center**). In the graphics window, click to specify the center point of the rectangle. Move the pointer and click to specify the midpoint of the first side. Also, the specified point defines the direction and distance of the second side. Next, specify the corner point to define the distance of the first side. This command creates the inclined as well as the horizontal rectangle.

Sketch techniques

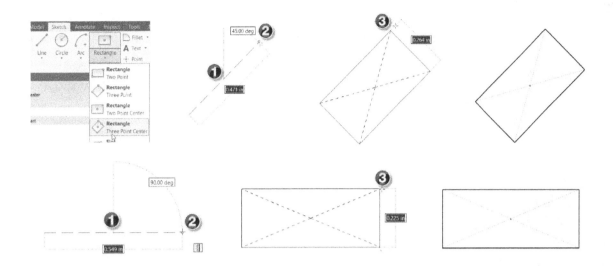

Creating Slots

In Inventor, you can create a straight and arc slots using five different commands: **Center to Center Slot, Overall Slot, Center Point Slot, Three Point Arc Slot, Center Point Arc Slot**.

Center to Center Slot

This command creates a straight slot by defining the centers of start and endcaps of the slot, and then defining its width. Activate this command (on the ribbon, click **Sketch > Create > Rectangle** drop-down > **Slot Center to Center**). Click to specify the start point of the slot. Next, move the pointer and click to specify the end point; the length and orientation of the slot are defined. Now, move the pointer outward and click to define the slot width.

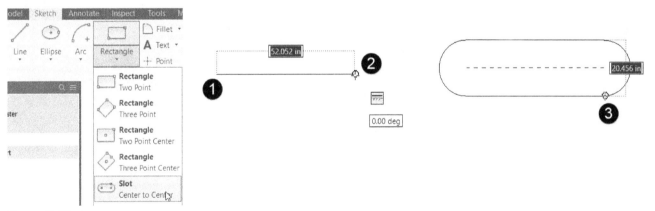

Overall Slot

This command creates a straight slot by defining its start, end, and width. Activate this command (on the ribbon, click **Sketch > Create > Rectangle** drop-down > **Slot Overall**). Specify the start and endpoints of the slot. Next, move the pointer and click to specify the slot width.

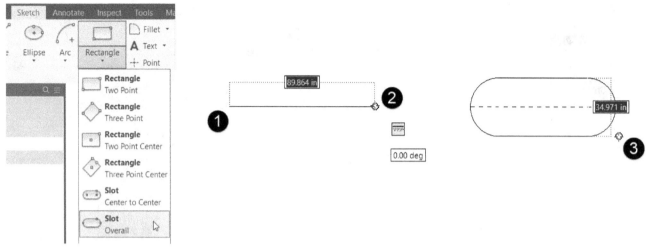

Center Point Slot

This command creates a straight slot by defining its centerpoint, endpoint, and width. Activate this command (on the ribbon, click **Sketch > Create > Rectangle** drop-down > **Slot Center Point**) and click to specify the centerpoint of the slot. Next, move the pointer and click to specify the centerpoint of the endcap; this defines the length and orientation of the slot. Now, move the pointer outward and click to define the slot width.

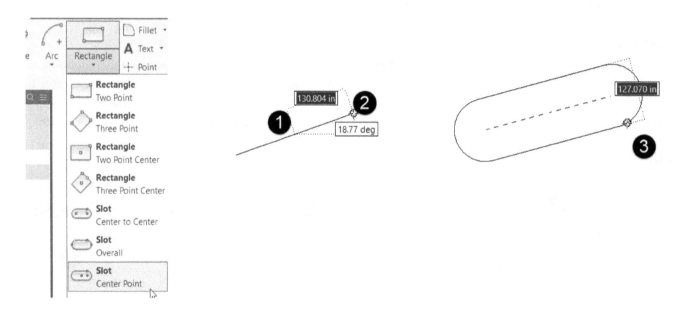

Three Point Arc Slot

This command is similar to the **Three Point Arc** command. Activate this command (on the ribbon, click **Sketch > Create > Rectangle** drop-down > **Slot Three Point Arc**) and specify the start and end points of the center arc of the slot. Next, you need to specify the third point of the center arc; this defines its radius. Now, move the pointer outward and click to define the slot width.

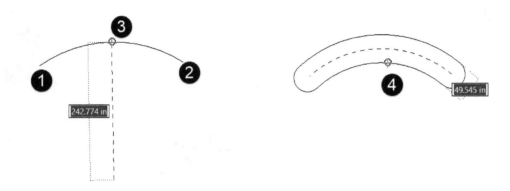

Center Point Arc Slot

This command works on the same principle as that of the **Center Point Arc** command. Activate this command (on the ribbon, click **Sketch > Create > Rectangle** drop-down > **Slot Center Point Arc**) and specify the center of the arc slot. Next, specify the start and end points of the center arc. Now, move the pointer outward and click to define the slot width.

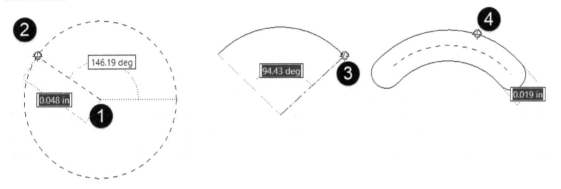

The Polygon command

This command provides a simple way to create a polygon with any number of sides. Activate this command (On the ribbon, click **Sketch > Create > Rectangle** drop-down **> Polygon**) and click in the graphics window to define the center of the polygon. As you move the pointer away from the center, you will see a preview of the polygon. To change the number of sides of the polygon, just click in the **Number of Sides** box on the dialog and enter a new number; the preview is updated.

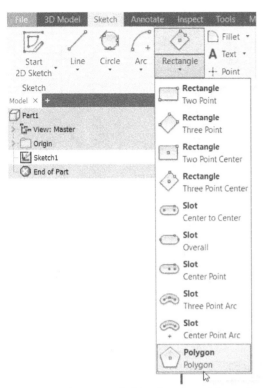

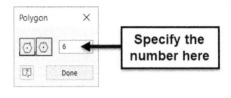

Now, you have to define the size of the polygon. On the **Polygon** dialog, there are two options to define the size of the polygon: **Inscribed** and **Circumscribed.** If you click the **Inscribed** option, a vertex of the polygon will be attached to the pointer. If you select **Circumscribed**, the pointer will be on one of the flat sides of the polygon. Click in the window to define the size and angle of the polygon. Click **Done** on the **Polygon** dialog to create a polygon.

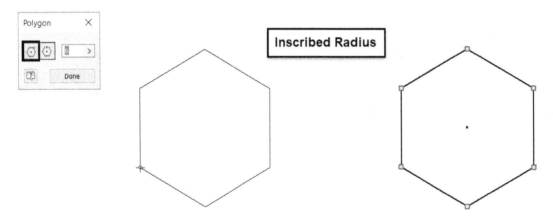

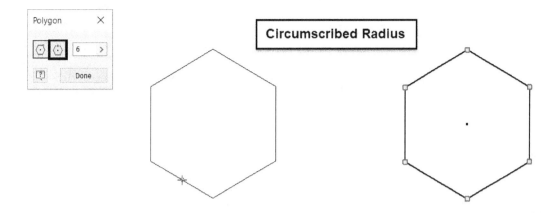

The Ellipse command

This command creates an ellipse using a center point, and major and minor axes. Activate this command (On the ribbon, click **Sketch > Create > Circle** drop-down **> Ellipse**). In the graphics window, click to define the center point of the ellipse. Move the pointer away from the center point and click to define the distance and orientation of the first axis. Next, move the pointer in the direction perpendicular to the first axis and click; the ellipse is created.

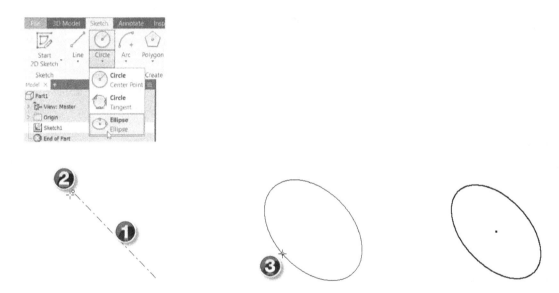

The Dimension command

It is generally considered a good practice to ensure that every sketch you create is fully constrained before creating solid features. The term, 'fully-constrained' means that the sketch has a definite shape and size. You can fully-constrain a sketch by using dimensions and constraints. You can add dimensions to a sketch by using the **Dimension** command. You can use this command to add all types of dimensions such as length, angle, and diameter and so on. This command creates a dimension based on the geometry you select. For instance, to dimension a circle, activate the **Dimension** command (On the ribbon, click **Sketch > Constrain > Dimension**), and then click on the circle. Next, move the pointer and click again to position the dimension; you will notice that the **Edit Dimension** box pops up. Type-in a value in this box, and then press Enter to update the dimension.

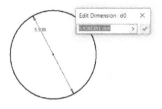 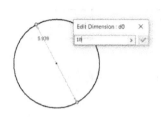 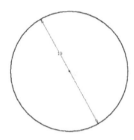

Linear Dimensions

To add dimension to a line, activate the **Dimension** command and select the line. Next, move the pointer in the vertical direction (or) right-click and select **Horizontal** from the menu; the horizontal dimension is created. Click to position the dimension.

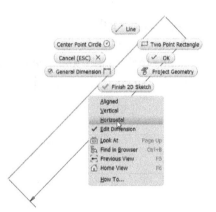 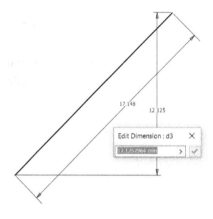

To create a vertical dimension, activate the **Dimension** command and select a line. Move the pointer in the horizontal direction (or) right-click and select **Vertical** from the shortcut menu; the vertical dimension is created. Click to position the dimension.

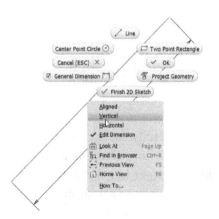 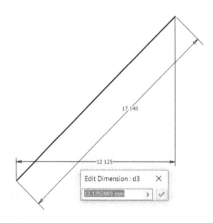

To create a dimension aligned to the selected line, right click and select **Aligned** from the shortcut menu. Next, position the dimension and edit its value.

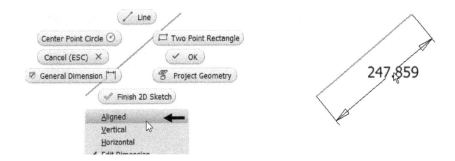

Angular Dimensions

Click the **Dimension** command on the **Constrain** panel of the **Sketch** tab, and then select two lines that are positioned at an angle to each other. Move the pointer between the selected lines and click to position the dimension. Next, type-in a value, and click the **OK** button.

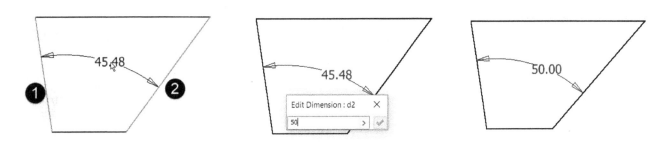

Adding Dimensions to an Arc

Inventor allows you to add five types of dimensions to an arc: Radius, Diameter, Arc Length, Arc angle, and Linear dimension.

Adding a Radius or Diameter or Arc Length dimension

To add a radius or diameter or arc length dimension to an arc, activate the **Dimension** command and select the arc. Next, right click and select **Dimension Type > Radius** or **Diameter** or **Arc Length**. Position the dimension and edit the dimension value.

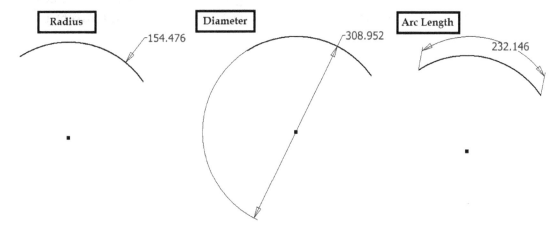

Adding a Linear dimension to the Arc

To add a linear dimension to an arc, activate the **Dimension** command and select its end points. Next, select the arc and position the linear dimension.

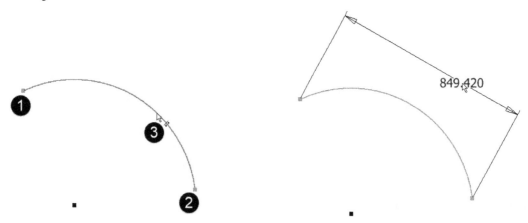

Adding an Angular dimension to an Arc

To add an angular dimension to an arc, activate the **Dimension** command and select the center point of the arc. Next, select the arc and position the angular dimension.

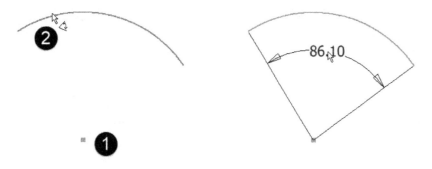

Over-constrained Sketch

When creating sketches for a solid or surface feature, Autodesk Inventor will not allow you to over-constrain the geometry. The term 'over-constrain' means adding more dimensions than required. The following figure shows a fully constrained sketch. If you add another dimension to this sketch (e.g. diagonal dimension), the **Create Linear Dimension** message pops up. It shows that the dimension over constrains the sketch. If you click **Accept**, then the dimension in the sketch will be displayed in brackets.

Constraints

The constraints are used to control the shape of a drawing by establishing relationships between the sketch elements. You can apply constraints to a sketch using the commands available on the **Constrain** panel of the **Sketch** ribbon.

Coincident Constraint

This constraint connects a point with another point. Click the **Coincident Constraint** button on the **Constrain** panel of the **Sketch** tab and select the points to be made coincident to each other. The selected points will be connected.

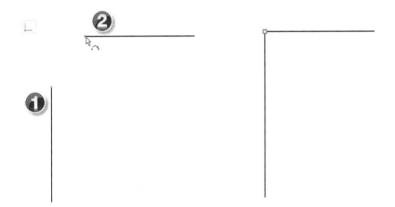

In addition to that, this constraint makes a vertex or a point to be on a line, curve, arc, or circle. Click the **Coincident Constraint** button on the **Constrain** panel and select a line, circle, arc, or curve. Next, select the point to be made coincident. The point will lie on the selected entity or its extension.

The **Coincident** constraint also forces a point or vertex to be aligned with the midpoint of a line. Activate the **Coincident Constraint** command and click on a point or vertex. Next, click on the midpoint of a line; the point will coincide with the midpoint of the line.

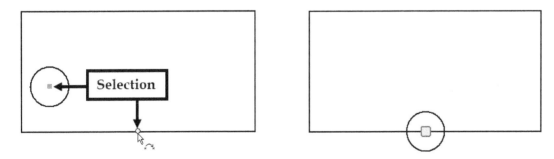

Horizontal Constraint

This constraint makes a line horizontal. Click the **Horizontal Constraint** button on the **Constrain** panel and select a free-to-move line; the line is made horizontal.

The **Horizontal Constraint** also aligns the two selected points horizontally. Click the **Horizontal Constraint** button on the **Constrain** panel and then select the points to align them horizontally.

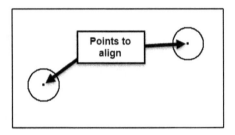 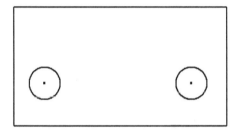

Vertical Constraint

This constraint makes a line vertical. Click the **Vertical Constraint** button on the **Constrain** panel and select an under-constrained line; the line is made vertical.

The **Vertical Constraint** also aligns the two selected points vertically. Click the **Vertical Constraint** button on the **Constrain** panel and then select the points to align vertically.

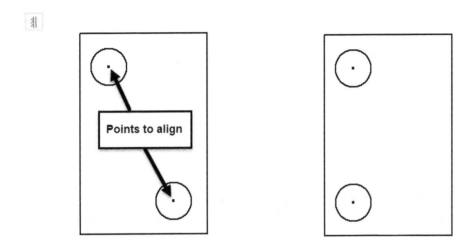

Concentric Constraint

This constraint makes the center points of two arcs, circles or ellipses coincident with each other. Click the **Concentric Constraint** button on the **Constrain** panel and select a circle or arc from the sketch. Select another circle or arc. The circles/arcs will be concentric to each other.

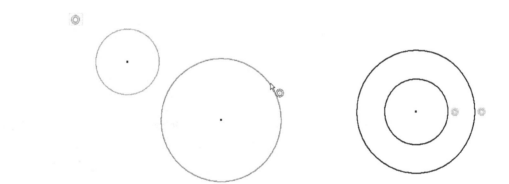

Equal

This constraint makes two lines equal in length.

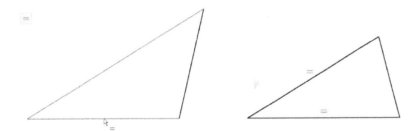

In addition to that, this constraint makes two circles or arcs equal in size.

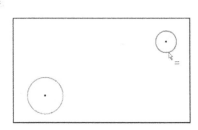
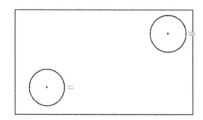

Collinear Constraint

This constraint forces a line to be collinear to another line. The lines are not required to touch each other. On the ribbon, click **Sketch > Constrain > Collinear Constraint**. Select the two lines, as shown. The second line will be collinear to the first line.

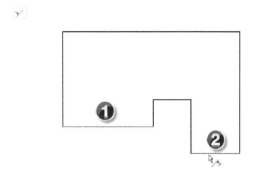
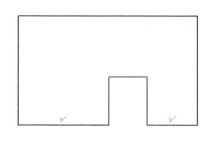

Tangent

This constraint makes an arc, circle, or line tangent to another arc or circle. On the **Constrain** panel, click the **Tangent** button and select a circle, arc, or line. Select another circle, arc, or line; both the elements become tangent to each other.

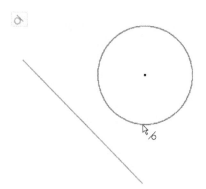
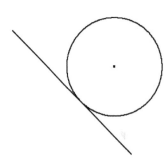

Parallel Constraint

This constraint makes two lines parallel to each other. Click the **Parallel Constraint** button on the **Constrain** panel and select two lines from the sketch. The under constrained line is made parallel to the constrained line. For example, if you select a line with the **Vertical Constraint** and a free to move line, the free-to-move line becomes parallel to the vertical line.

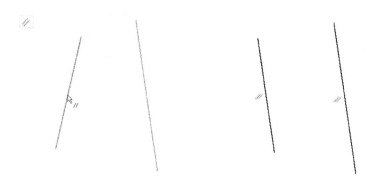

Perpendicular Constraint

This constraint makes two lines perpendicular to each other. Click the **Perpendicular Constraint** button on the **Constrain** panel and select two lines from the sketch. The two lines will be made perpendicular to each other.

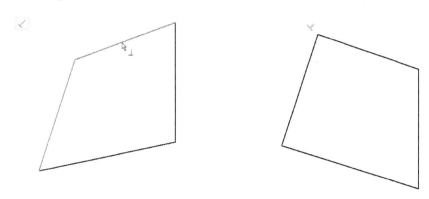

Symmetric

This command makes two objects symmetric about a line. The objects will have same size, position and orientation about a line. Activate this command (on the ribbon, **Sketch > Constrain > Symmetric)** and click on the first object. Next, click on the second object, and then select the symmetry line. The two objects will be made symmetric about the symmetry line.

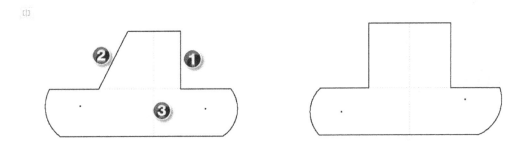

You can continue selecting the objects to be made symmetric about the previously selected symmetry line.

Constraint Settings

The **Constraint Settings** dialog helps you to specify settings related to infer constraints and dimensions. Infer constraints are applied between the sketch elements immediately after they are created. The type of constraints applied between the sketch elements depends on their position and orientation. To open the **Constraint Settings** dialog, click **Sketch > Constrain > Constraint Settings** on the ribbon.

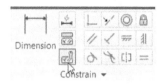

The Inference tab

The inference options are available on the **Inference** tab of the **Constraint Settings** dialog. Click this tab on the **Constraint Settings** dialog and check the **Infer Constraints** option, if not already checked. Next, check the constraints in the **Selection for Constraint Inference** section that are to be created while creating the sketch. By default, all the constraints are checked.

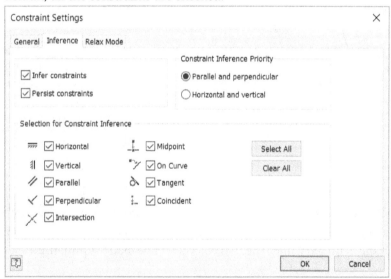

Under the **Constraint Inference Priority** section, specify the priority of the constraints to be created between two sketch elements. For example, check the **Parallel and Perpendicular** option from the **Constraint Inference Priority** section. Next, create a horizontal line and move the pointer vertically upward. Notice that Inventor tries to create the **Perpendicular** constraint between the horizontal line and the new line. However, if you check the **Horizontal and vertical** option, Inventor will create the **Vertical** constraint between the horizontal line and the new line.

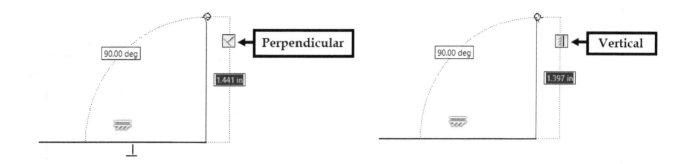

Click **OK** to close the dialog.

Show/Hide All Constraints

As constraints are created, they can be viewed using the **Show All Constraints** option. To view all the constraints of a sketch, right click in the graphics window and select **Show All Constraints**. When dealing with complicated sketches involving numerous relations, you can turn off all the constraints. To do this, right click in the graphics window and select **Hide All Constraints**.

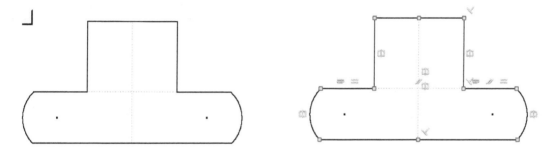

Adding Dimensions and Constraints Automatically

Inventor has a command to add dimensions and constraints to the sketch automatically. On the ribbon, click

Sketch > Constrain panel > **Automatic Dimensions and Constraints** ⊢ . On the **Auto Dimension** dialog, the number of dimensions required to fully-constrain the sketch is displayed. Click **Apply** on the **Auto Dimension** dialog to apply the dimensions. Click **Done** if you are satisfied with the dimension. Otherwise, click **Remove** to erase all the automatic dimensions.

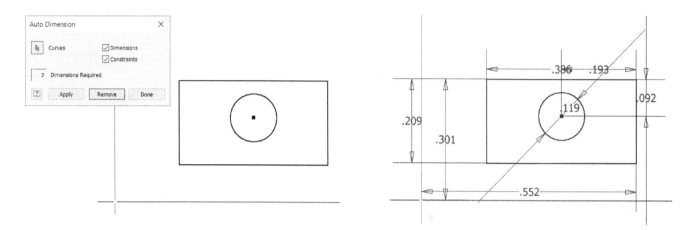

The Construction Command

This command converts a sketch element into a construction element. Construction elements support you to create a sketch of desired shape and size. To convert a sketch element to a construction element, click on it and click **Sketch > Format > Construction** on the ribbon. You can also convert it back to a sketch element by clicking on it and deselecting the **Construction** button on the **Format** panel.

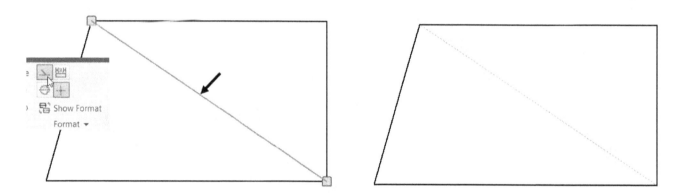

The Centerline Command

This command converts a line into a centerline. The centerline can be used as the axis of revolution while creating a revolved feature. Select a line to convert it into a centerline and click the **Centerline** button (on the ribbon, click **Sketch > Format > Centerline**). You can also create centerlines directly by activating the **Centerline** command.

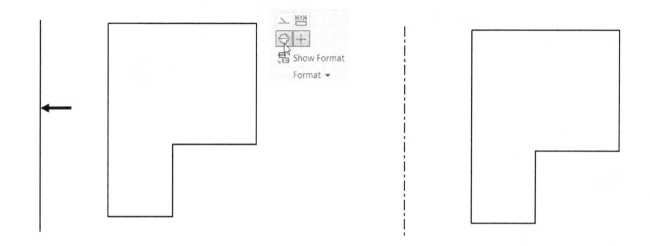

⌐ The Fillet command

This command rounds a sharp corner created by intersection of two lines, arcs, circles, and rectangle or polygon vertices. Activate this command (On the ribbon, click **Sketch > Create > Fillet**) and type-in a radius value in the **Radius** box on the **2D Fillet** dialog. Next, select the elements' ends to be filleted. The elements to be filleted are not required to touch each other. Keep on selecting the elements of the sketch; the fillets are added at the corners at which two selected elements intersect. Also, notice that the fillets are created with equal radius and a dimension is added to only one fillet.

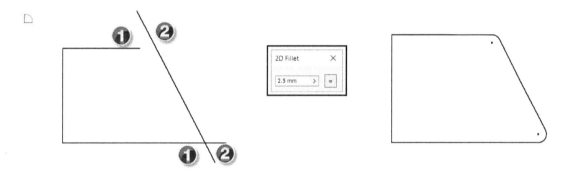

If you want to create a fillet with a different radius, then deselect the **Equal** icon on the **2D Fillet** dialog. Next, type-in a new value in the **Radius** box, and then select the corners to be filleted. Separate dimensions are added to each of the fillets. You can change the fillet radii individually by double clicking on the dimensions.

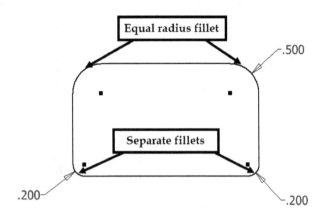

⬜ The Chamfer command

This command places an angled line at the intersection of two nonparallel lines. It can create a chamfer using anyone of three different options: **Equidistant**, **Two distances**, and **Distance and Angle**. Activate this command (On the ribbon, click **Sketch > Create > Fillet** drop-down **> Chamfer**) and select the elements' ends to be chamfered. By default, **Equidistant** icon is selected to define the chamfer. Type-in the chamfer distance in the

Distance box and click **OK**. By default, the **Dimension** ⬜icon is selected on the **2D Chamfer** dialog. As a result, the dimensions are added to chamfer. Deselect this icon if you do not want to add a dimension.

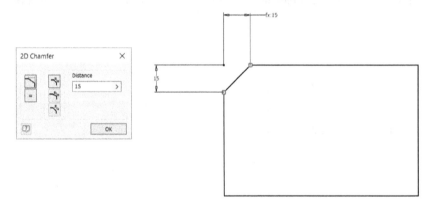

On the **2D Chamfer** dialog, click the **Two Distances** icon and type-in the chamfer distances in the **Distance1** and **Distance2 boxes**. Next, select the corner to be chamfered and click **OK**.

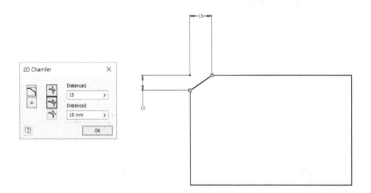

On the **2D Chamfer** dialog, click **Distance and Angle** icon and type-in the chamfer distance and angle in the **Distance** and **Angle** boxes, respectively. Next, select the corner to be chamfered and click **OK**.

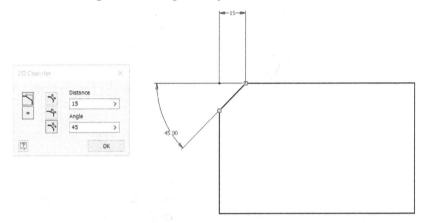

The Extend command

This command extends elements such as lines, arcs, and curves until they touch the another element called the boundary edge. Activate this command (On the ribbon, click **Sketch > Modify > Extend**) and click on the element to extend. It will extend up to the next element.

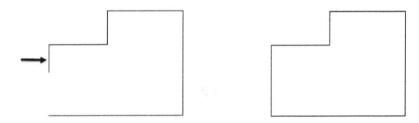

The Trim command

This command trims the end of an element back to the intersection of another element. Activate this command (On the ribbon, click **Sketch > Modify > Trim**) and click on the element or elements to trim. You can also drag the pointer across the elements to trim.

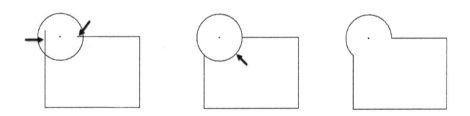

The Offset command

This command creates a parallel copy of a selected element or chain of elements. Activate this command (On the ribbon click **Sketch > Modify > Offset**) and select an element or chain of elements to offset. After selecting the element(s), move the pointer in the outward or inward direction, type-in a value in the **Distance** box, and press Enter. The parallel copy of the elements will be created.

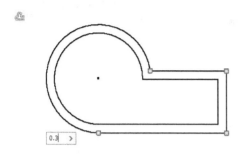

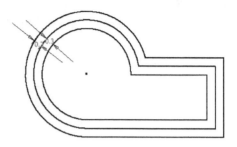

The Move command

This command relocates one or more elements from one position in the sketch to any other position that you specify. Activate this command from the **Modify** panel, and then click on the elements to move. Next, click the **Base Point** button and select a base point; a message box appears if there are any constraints or dimensions associated with the selected sketch element. Click **Yes** to relax the dimensions and constraints associated with the object. Move the pointer and click at a new location. Click **Done**.

The Copy command

The **Copy** command can be used to copy and move the selected elements.

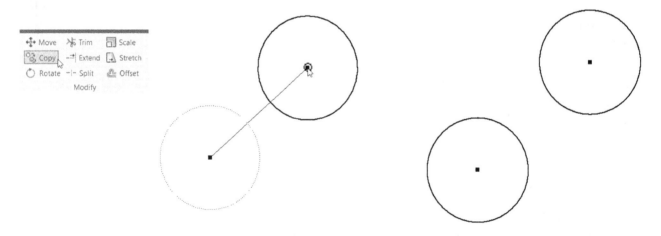

The Rotate command

This command rotates the selected elements to any position. Activate this command from the **Modify** panel, and then select the elements to rotate. Next, you must define a center point and a point from which the object will be rotated. Move the pointer and click to define the rotation angle. You can use the **Copy** option on the **Rotate** dialog to copy and rotate the selected elements. Click **Done**.

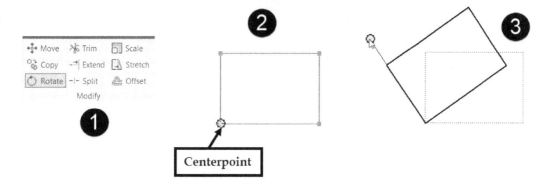

The Scale command

This command increases or decreases the size of elements in a sketch. Activate this command from **Modify** panel, and then select the elements to scale. After selecting the elements, click the **Base Point** button and select a base point. You can then scale the size of the selected elements by moving the pointer and clicking (or) entering a scale factor value in the **Scale Factor** field on the dialog.

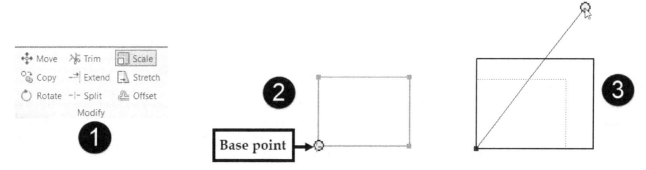

The Stretch command

This command stretches the selected geometry using a base point. Activate this command (On the ribbon, click **Sketch > Modify > Stretch**), click the **Select** selection button on the **Stretch** dialog, and select the elements to be stretched. Next, click the **Base Point** selection button on the **Stretch** dialog and select the point, as shown. Autodesk Inventor pops-up a dialog, showing, "The geometry being edited is constrained to other geometry. Would you like those constraints removed?". Click the **Yes** button, drag the base point, and then click to stretch the part geometry. Click **Done** after stretching.

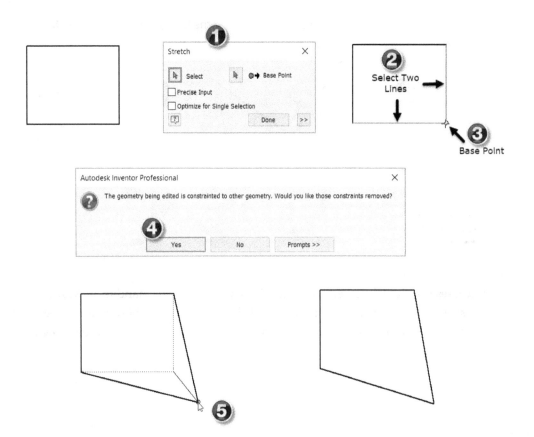

Circular Sketch Pattern

This command creates circular pattern of the selected sketch elements. Activate the **Circular Pattern** command (on the ribbon, click **Sketch > Pattern > Circular**) and select the sketch elements to be patterned circularly. On the **Circular Pattern** dialog, click the **Axis** button and select a point around which the sketch elements will be patterned. Next, type-in a value in the **Count** box to define the instance count of thee pattern. Next, specify the total angle in the **Angle** box. By default, it is 360-degrees and you can change its value as per your requirement.

Click the expand button located at the bottom right corner of the dialog and notice the three options: **Supress**, **Associative**, and **Fitted**.

The **Fitted** option helps you to specify the total angle of the circular pattern. If you uncheck this option, the value that you enter in the **Angle** box will be taken as the angle between the instances.

The **Associative** option creates a link between the source object and the patterned instances. If you modify the source object, the patterned instances will be modified, automatically. In addition to that, you cannot delete the instances of the pattern.

The **Supress** option helps you to supress instances.

Click **OK** to create a circular sketch pattern. Use the **Trim** command to erase the unwanted portions of the sketch.

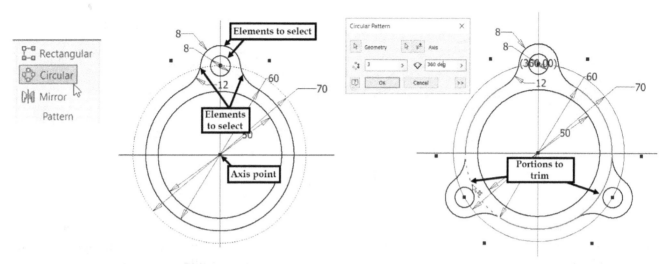

Rectangular Sketch Pattern

This command creates rectangular pattern of the selected sketch elements. Activate the **Rectangular Pattern** command (on the ribbon, click **Sketch > Pattern > Rectangle**) and select the sketch elements to pattern. On the **Rectangular Pattern** dialog, click the cursor icon in the **Direction 1** section and select a line to define the first direction. You can click the **Flip** icon to reverse the direction in which the pattern is created. Next, type-in values in the **Count** and **Spacing** boxes. Likewise, specify the **Direction 2** settings and click **OK**.

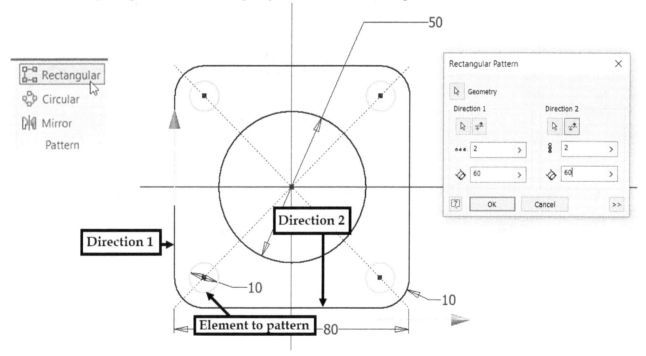

The Mirror command

This command creates a mirror image of the selected elements. It also creates the **Symmetric** constraint between the original and mirrored elements. Activate this command from the **Pattern** panel, and then select the elements to mirror. Next, click the **Mirror Line** button and select a line to define the mirror-line. Click **Apply** and **Done** on the **Mirror** dialog.

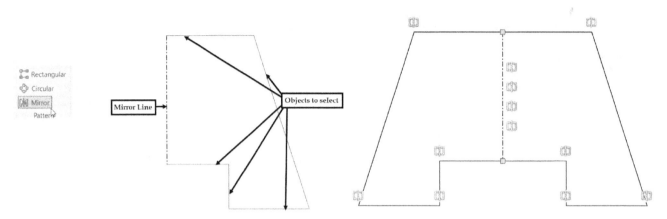

Creating Splines

Splines are non-uniform curves, which are used to create smooth shapes. In Inventor, you can create a smooth spline curve using two commands: **Control Vertex Spline** and **Interpolation Spline**.

Control Vertex Spline

The **Control Vertex Spline** command helps you to create a spline by defining various points called as control vertices. Activate this command (on the ribbon, click **Sketch > Create > Line** drop-down > **Spline Control Vertex**). In the graphics window, click to specify the first control vertex. Move the pointer and specify the second vertex. Likewise, specify the other control vertices. As you define the control vertices, dotted lines are created connecting them. Also, a spline will be created. Press Enter to complete the spline.

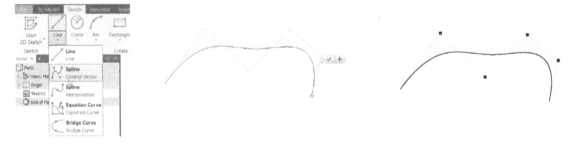

You can also add new control vertices to the spline. To do this, right-click on the spline and select **Insert Vertex** from the menu. Click on the desired position to place the new vertex. Now, you can modify the shape and size of the spline by dragging the control vertices. You can also add dimensions and constraints to the control vertices and dotted lines.

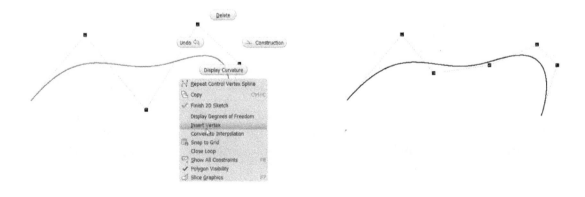

Interpolation Spline

The **Interpolation Spline** command creates a smooth spline passing through a series of points called fit points. Activate this command, by clicking **Sketch > Create > Line** drop-down **> Spline Interpolation**. In the graphics window, click to specify the first point of the spline. Move the pointer and specify the second point of the spline. Likewise, specify the other points of the spline, and then press Enter to create the spline. The endpoints are square shaped, whereas the fit points along the curve are diamond shape.

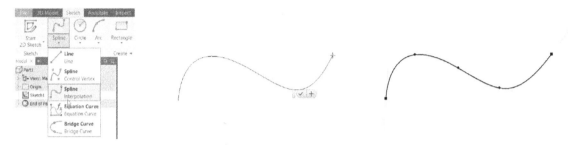

You can add a new fit point on the spline. To do this, right-click on the spline and select **Insert point** from the menu. Click on the desired position to place the new point. You can click and drag the fit points to reposition them. Also, it changes the shape of the spline.

Examples

Example 1 (Millimeters)

In this tutorial you will draw the sketch shown below.

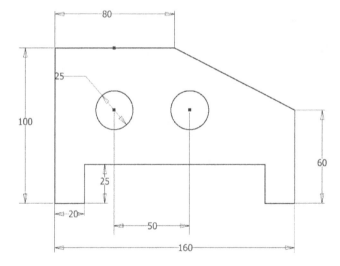

1. Start **Autodesk Inventor 2019** by double-clicking the **Autodesk Inventor 2019** icon on your desktop.
2. To start a new part file, click **Get Started > Launch > New** on the ribbon.
3. On the **Create New File** dialog, click the **Metric** folder under **Templates**.
4. Click the **Standard(mm).ipt** icon under the **Part – Create 2D and 3D Objects** section.

Sketch techniques

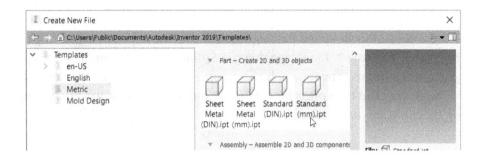

5. Click the **Create** button on the **Create New File** dialog.

A new model window appears.

Starting a Sketch

1. To start a sketch, click **3D Model > Sketch > Start 2D Sketch** on the ribbon. Click on the XZ plane. The sketch starts.

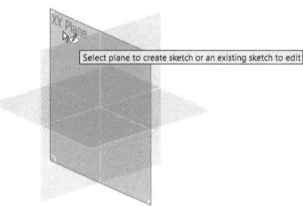

2. Click **Sketch > Create > Line** on the ribbon. Click on the origin point to define the first point of the line.

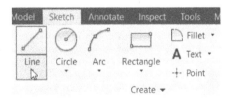

3. Move the pointer along the horizontal axis (thick axis) and toward right.
4. Click to define the endpoint of the line.
5. Move the pointer vertically upwards. Click to create the second line.

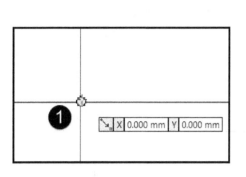 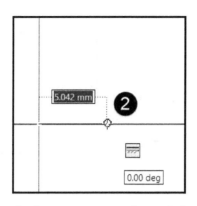 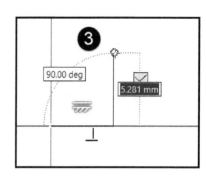

6. Create a closed loop by selecting points in the sequence, as shown below.

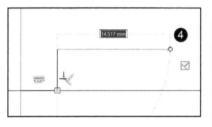 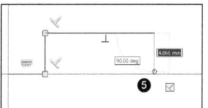 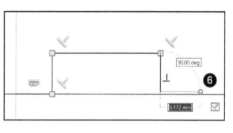

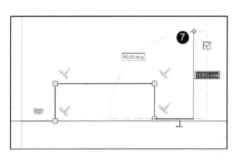 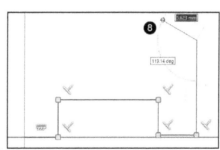 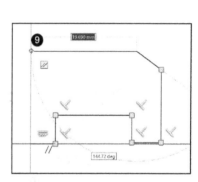

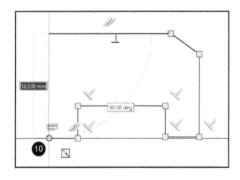

Adding Constraints

1. Click **Sketch > Constrain > Collinear Constraint** on the ribbon, and then click on the two horizontal lines at the bottom; they become collinear.

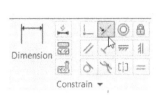

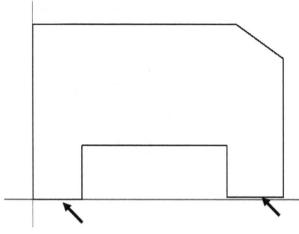

2. Click **Sketch > Constrain > Equal** 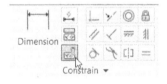 on the ribbon and click on the two horizontal lines at the bottom; they become equal in length.

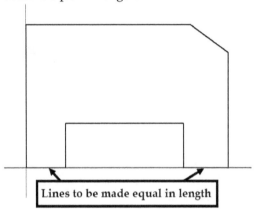

Lines to be made equal in length

Adding Dimensions

1. On the ribbon, click **Sketch > Constrain > Constraint Settings**. On the **Constraint Settings** dialog, click the **General** tab and check the **Edit dimension when created** option. Click **OK** to close the dialog.

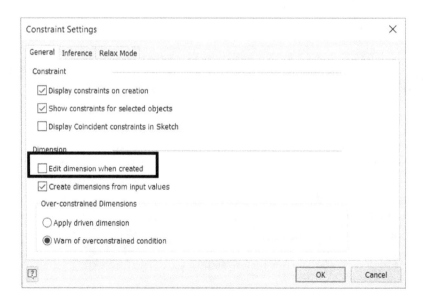

Sketch techniques

2. Click **Sketch > Constraint > Dimension** on the ribbon and click on the left and right vertical lines. Move the mouse pointer downward and click to locate the dimension.
3. Type-in **160** in the **Edit dimension** box and press Enter.

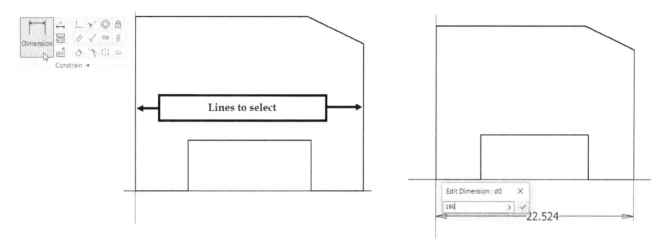

4. On the Navigate Bar, click **Zoom > Zoom All**; the sketch is fit in the graphics window.
5. Click on the lower left horizontal line. Move the mouse pointer downward and click to locate the dimension.
6. Type-in **20** in the dimension box and press Enter.

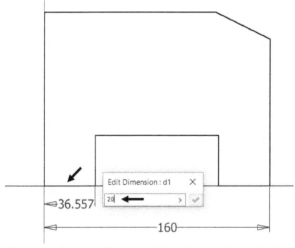

7. Click on the small vertical line located at the left side. Move the mouse pointer towards right and click to position the dimension.
8. Type-in **25** in the dimension box and press Enter.

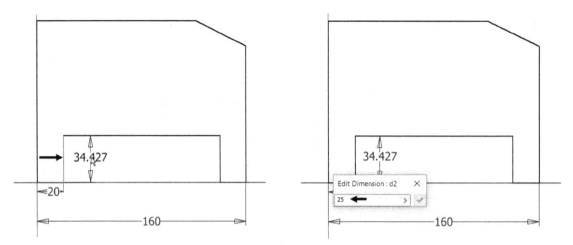

9.   Create other dimensions in the sequence, as shown below. Press Esc to deactivate the **Dimension** command.

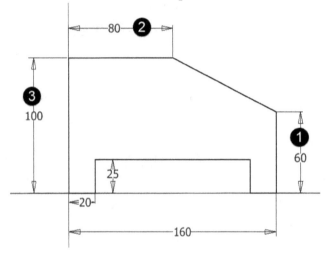

10. On the ribbon, click **Sketch > Create > Circle Center Point**. Click inside the sketch region to define the center point of the circle. Move the mouse pointer and click to define the diameter. Likewise, create another circle.

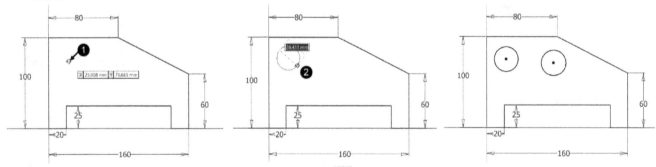

11. On the ribbon, click **Sketch > Constrain > Horizontal**. Click on the center points of the two circles to make them horizontally aligned.

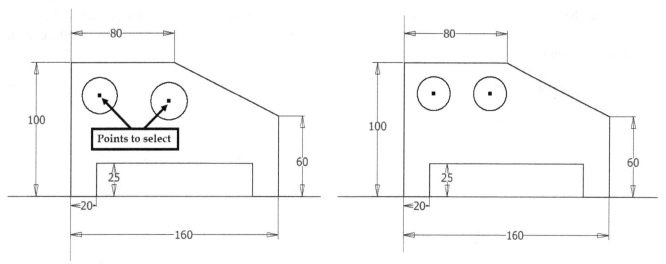

12. Select the center point of anyone of the circle and the corner point, as shown; the circles are aligned horizontally with the corner point.

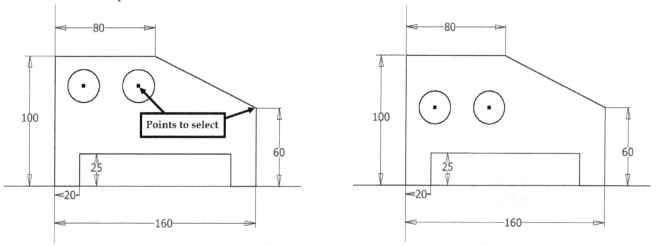

13. On the ribbon, click **Sketch > Constrain > Vertical**. Click on the center point of the left circle and the midpoint of the top horizontal line; the left circle is aligned vertically with the midpoint of the top horizontal line.

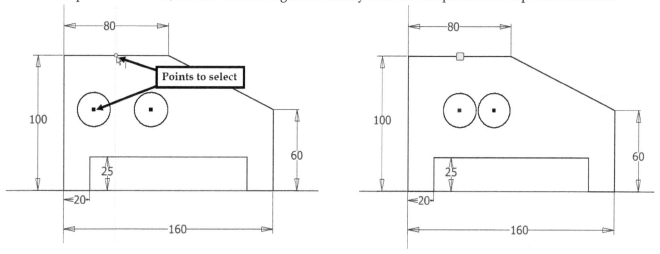

14. On the ribbon, click **Sketch > Constrain > Equal**, and then click on the two circles. The diameters of the circles will become equal.

15. Activate the **Dimension** command and click on anyone of the circles. Move the mouse pointer and click to position the dimension. Type 25 in the dimension box and press Enter. Create a dimension between the circles, as shown below.

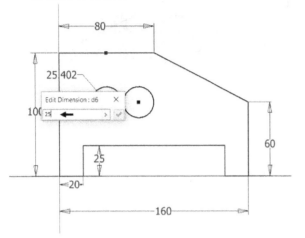 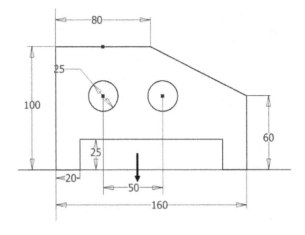

Finishing the Sketch and Saving it

1. On the ribbon, click **Sketch > Exit > Finish Sketch** to complete the sketch.

2. Click the **Save** icon on the **Quick Access Toolbar**. Define the location and file name and click **Save** to save the part file.

3. Click **Close** on the top right corner of the graphics window to close the part file.

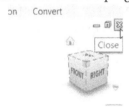

Example 2 (Inches)

In this tutorial you will draw the sketch shown next.

Sketch techniques

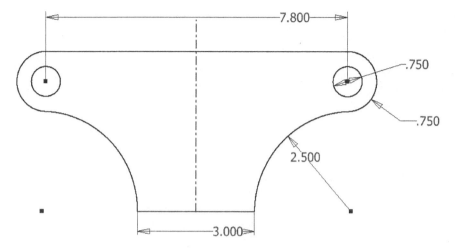

1. Start **Autodesk Inventor 2019** by double-clicking the **Autodesk Inventor 2019** icon on your desktop.
2. To start a new part file, click **Get Started > Launch > New** on the ribbon.
3. On the **Create New File** dialog, click the **Templates** folder.
4. Click the **Standard.ipt** icon under the **Part – Create 2D and 3D Objects** section.

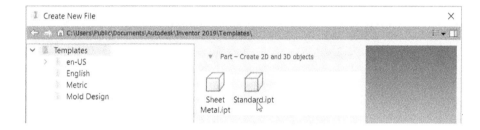

5. Click the **Create** button on the **Create New File** dialog.

Starting a Sketch

1. To start a sketch, click **3D Model > Sketch > Start 2D Sketch** on the ribbon. Click on the XY plane. The sketch starts.

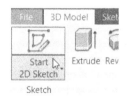
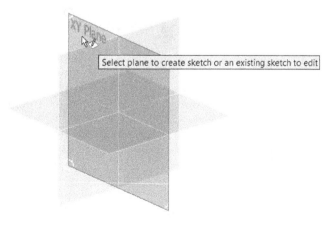

2. Activate the **Line** command (On the ribbon, click **Sketch > Create > Line**).

3. Click in the second quadrant of the coordinate system to define the start point of the profile. Drag the pointer horizontally and click to define the endpoint.

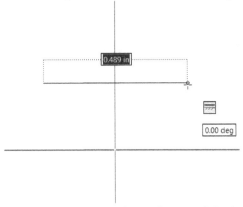

4. Take the pointer to the endpoint of the line. Next, press and hold the left mouse button and drag the pointer along the vertical dotted line. Move the pointer towards right, as shown. Release the left mouse button to create an arc normal to the horizontal line.

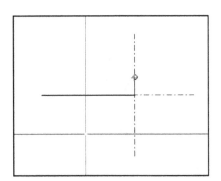 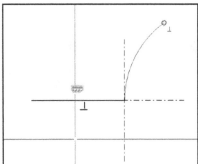 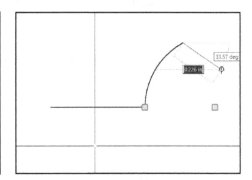

5. Take the pointer to the endpoint of the arc. Next, press and hold the left mouse button and drag it towards right, and then upwards. Release the left mouse button when a vertical dotted line appears, as shown.

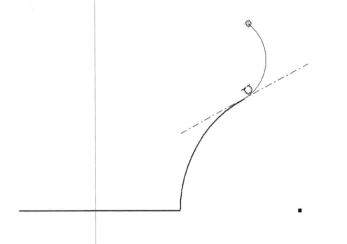 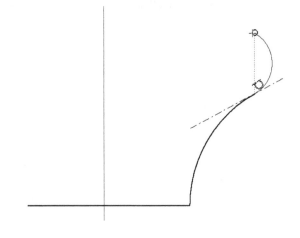

6. Move the pointer toward left and click to create a horizontal line.

Sketch techniques

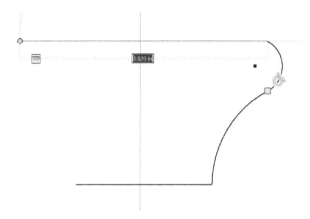

7. On the ribbon, click **Sketch > Create > Arc drop-down > Arc Three Point** 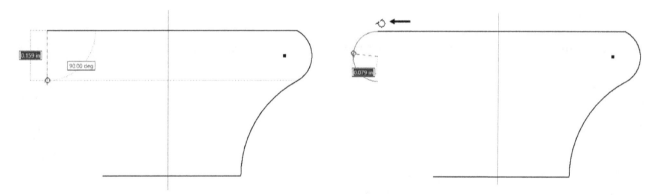 . Select the end point of the line and move it downward and click when a vertical dotted line appears, as shown. Move the pointer towards left and click when the Tangent constraint symbol appears.

8. Make sure that the **Arc** command is active. Select the end point of the last arc and move the pointer downward and click on the start point of the lower horizontal line. Move the pointer upward right, and then click to close the sketch. Click the right mouse button and click **OK**.

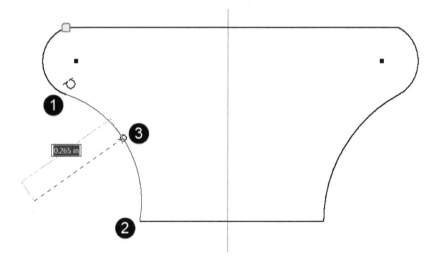

9. Click **Sketch > Create > Circle Center Point** on the ribbon. Draw a circle inside the closed sketch as shown.

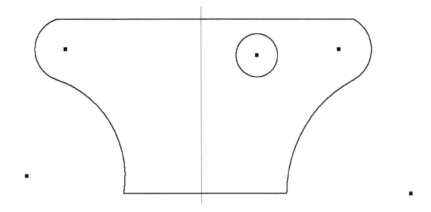

10. Click **Sketch > Constrain > Concentric Constraint** on the ribbon.

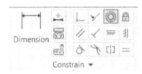

11. Click on the circle and small arc on the upper right. The circle and arc are made concentric.

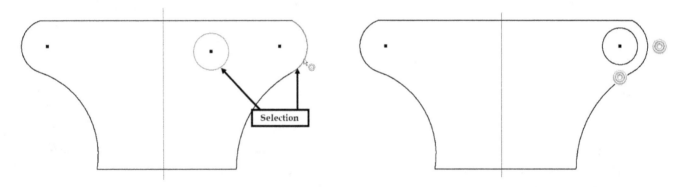

12. Likewise, create another circle concentric to the small arc located on the left side.

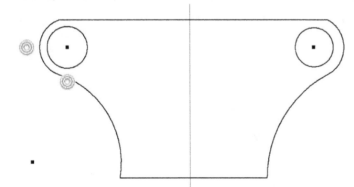

13. On the ribbon, click **Sketch > Format > Centerline** . Next, activate the **Line** command and create a vertical line starting from the sketch origin.

Sketch techniques

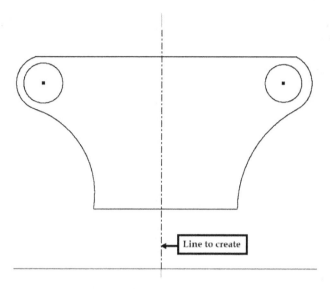

Line to create

14. On the ribbon, click **Sketch > Constrain > Symmetric**.

15. Click on the large arcs on both sides of the centerline. Next, select the centerline; arcs are made symmetric about the centerline.

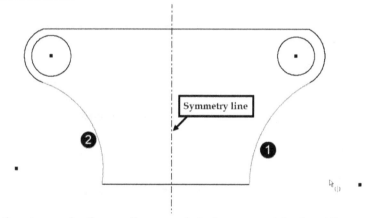

Symmetry line

16. Likewise, make the small arcs and circles symmetric about the centerline.

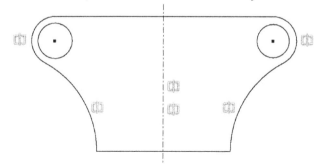

17. On the ribbon, click **Sketch > Constraint > Coincident Constraint**, and then select the bottom horizontal line and sketch origin.

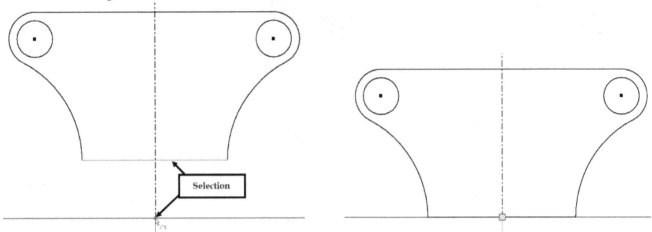

18. Activate the **Dimension** command and apply dimensions to the sketch in the sequence, as shown below.

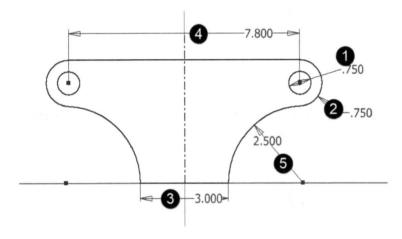

19. On the Navigation pane, click **Zoom > Zoom All** to fit the drawing in the graphics window. The sketch is fully constrained and all the sketch elements are displayed in blue color.
20. Click **Finish Sketch** on the ribbon to complete the sketch.
21. To save the file, click **File > Save**.
22. On the **Save As** dialog, specify the location of the file and type-in **C1_Example2** in the **File name** box and click the **Save** button.
23. To close the file, click **File > Close > Close All**.

Example 3 (Millimeters)

In this tutorial you will draw the sketch shown below.

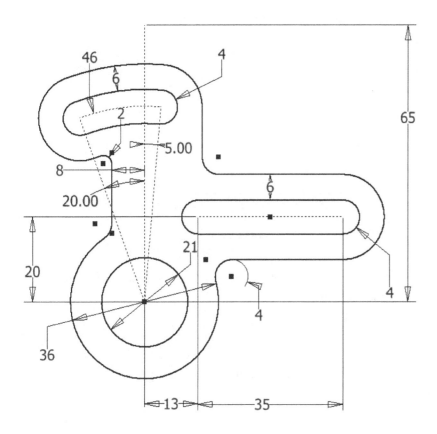

1. Start **Autodesk Inventor 2019** by double-clicking the **Autodesk Inventor 2019** icon on your desktop.
2. To start a new part file, click **Get Started > Launch > New** on the ribbon.
3. On the **Create New File** dialog, click the **Metric** folder under **Templates**.
4. Click the **Standard(mm).ipt** icon under the **Part – Create 2D and 3D Objects** section.

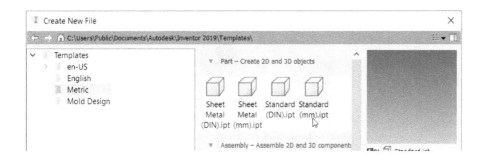

5. Click the **Create** button on the **Create New File** dialog.

A new model window appears.

Starting a Sketch

1. To start a sketch, click **3D Model > Sketch > Start 2D Sketch** on the ribbon. Click on the XZ plane. The sketch starts.

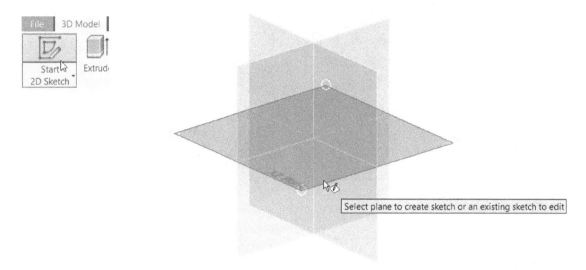

2. Click **Sketch > Create > Circle Center Point** on the ribbon. Click on the origin point to define the center point of the circle. Move the pointer outward and click to create a circle.

3. Likewise, create another circle with the origin point as its center.

4. On the ribbon, click **Sketch > Constrain > Dimension** and select the inner circle. Place the dimension and type-in 21 in the **Edit Dimension** box. Click the green check; the size of the outer circle is adjusted automatically.

5. On the Navigate Bar, click Zoom, press and hold the left mouse button, and drag the pointer upward; sketch is zoomed out. Right click and select **OK**.

6. On the ribbon, click **Sketch > Create > Rectangle** drop-down > **Slot Center Point Arc** ⌣. Select the sketch origin to define the center point of the arc, and then define the start and end points of the arc, as shown. Move the pointer outward and click to define the slot width.

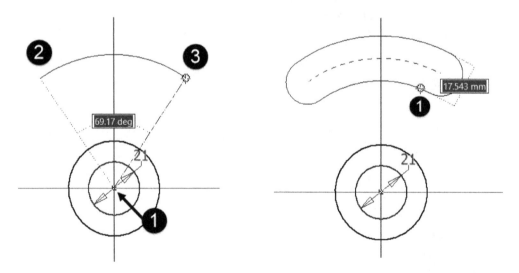

7. On the ribbon, click **Sketch > Create > Rectangle** drop-down > **Slot Center to Center** ⬭. Specify the center points of the endcaps, and then move the pointer outward and click to define its width. Right click and select **OK**.

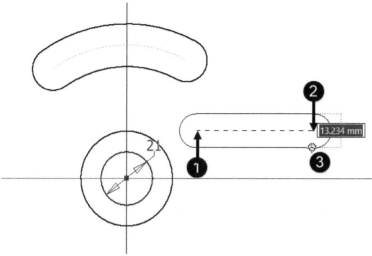

8. On the ribbon, click **Sketch > Format > Construction**, and then create a vertical line starting from the sketch origin. Likewise, create two more lines passing through the center points of the slot. Click on the **Construction** icon on the Format panel to deactivate it.

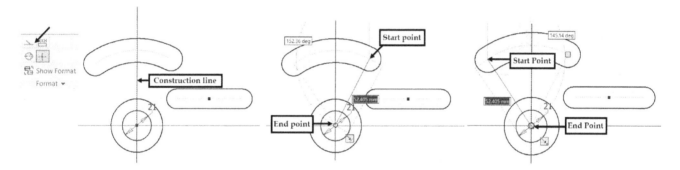

9. On the ribbon, click **Sketch > Constrain > Dimension**. Select the vertical construction line and the right construction line. Move the pointer between the two lines and click to place the dimension. Type-in 5 in the Edit dimension box, and then click the green check.
10. Likewise, create another angled dimension between the vertical and left construction lines.

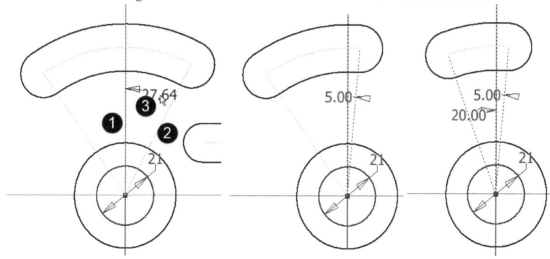

11. Add remaining dimensions to the sketch, as shown.

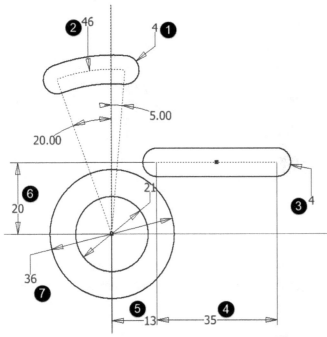

12. On the ribbon, click **Sketch > Modify > Offset** . Select the arc slot, move the pointer outward, type 6, and press Enter. Likewise, offset the straight slot by 6 mm distance.

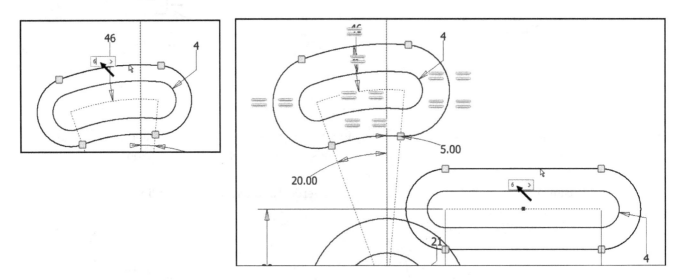

13. Select the vertical construction line with the **Offset** command still active. Move the pointer toward left, type 8 and press Enter. Right click and select **OK**.

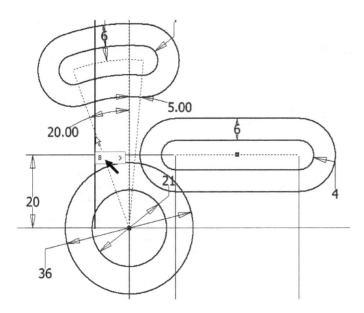

14. On the ribbon, click **Sketch > Create > Line**. Specify the start point on the offset of the arc slot, as shown. Move the pointer vertically downward and click on the offset of the straight slot.

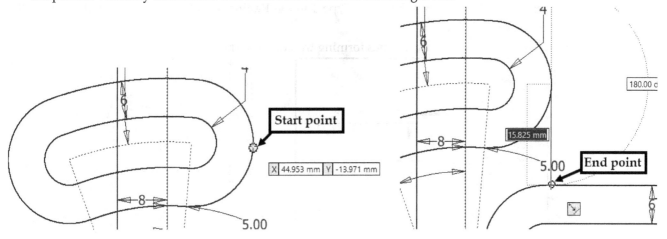

15. On the ribbon, click **Sketch > Modify > Trim** and click on the portions of the sketch, as shown. Right click and select **OK**.

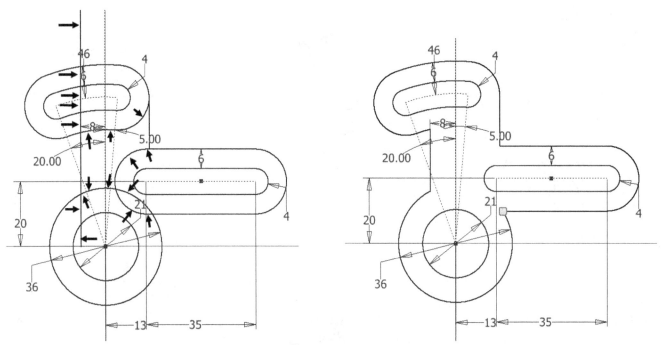

16. On the ribbon, click **Sketch > Create > Fillet**⌐. Type 4 in the **Radius** box of the **2D Fillet** dialog. Select the entities at the three corners, as shown.

17. Type 2 in the **Radius** box and select the entities forming the corner, a shown.

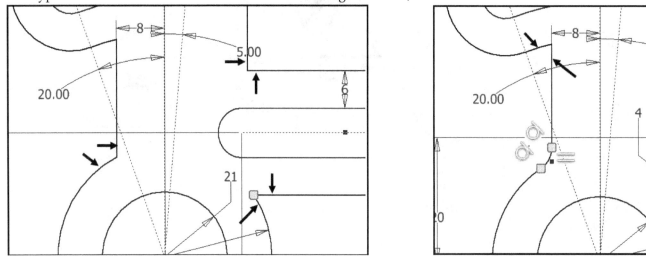

18. On the ribbon, click **Sketch > Constrain > Tangent**. Apply the tangent constraint between the set of entities, as shown.

Sketch techniques

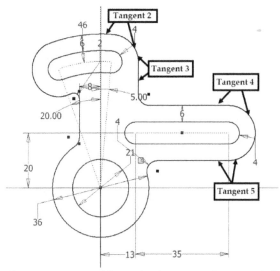

The sketch turns blue which means that it is fully defined. However, the status shows that 1 dimension is still needed to fully define the sketch.

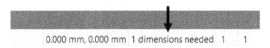

0.000 mm, 0.000 mm 1 dimensions needed 1   1

19. Add dimension to the vertical construction line; the status bar now displays the **Fully Constrained** message.
20. Click **Finish Sketch** on the ribbon to complete the sketch.
21. To save the file, click **File > Save**.
22. On the **Save As** dialog, specify the location of the file and type-in **C1_Example3** in the **File name** box and click the **Save** button.
23. To close the file, click **File > Close > Close All**.

Questions

1. What is the procedure to create sketches in Inventor?

2. List any two sketch *Constraints* in Inventor.

3. Which command allows you to apply dimensions to a sketch automatically?

4. Describe two methods to create circles.

5. How do you define the shape and size of a sketch?

6. How do you create a tangent arc using the **Line** command?

7. Which command is used to apply multiple types of dimensions to a sketch?

8. List the commands to create arcs?

9. List the commands to create slots?

10. What are inferred constraints?

Exercises

Exercise 1

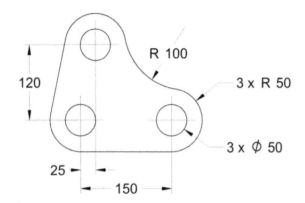

Exercise 2

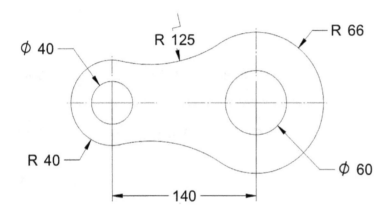

Exercise 3

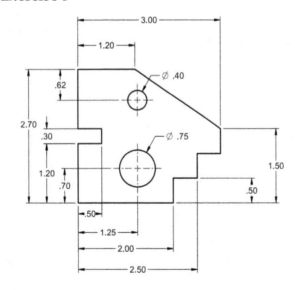

Chapter 3: Extrude and Revolve Features

Extrude and revolve features are used to create basic and simple parts. Most of the time, they form the base for complex parts as well. These features are easy to create and require a single sketch. Now, you will learn the commands to create these features.

In this chapter, you will learn to:
- Create *Extrude* and *Revolve* features in the part model
- Create Work Planes
- Work with additional options in the *Extrude* and *Revolve* commands

Extruded Features

Extruding is the process of taking a two-dimensional profile and converting it into 3D model by giving it some thickness. A simple example of this would be taking a circle and converting it into a cylinder. Once you have created a sketch profile or profiles you want to *Extrude*, activate the **Extrude** command (On the ribbon click **3D Model > Create > Extrude**); the sketch is selected, automatically. Click inside the sketch profile, if not already selected. Type-in a value in the **Distance** box to specify the thickness of the *Extruded* feature.

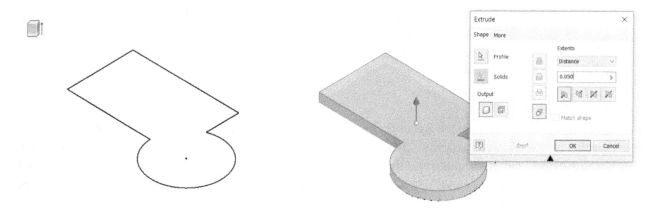

You can click the **Symmetric** icon on the dialog to add equal thickness on both sides of the sketch.

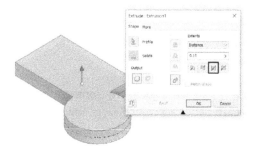

On the dialog, click **OK** to complete the *Extruded* feature.

Revolved Features

Revolve is the process of taking a two-dimensional profile and revolving it about a centerline to create a 3D geometry (shapes that are axially symmetric). While creating a sketch for the *Revolved* feature, it is important to think about the cross-sectional shape that will define the 3D geometry once it is revolved about an axis. For instance, the following geometry has a hole in the center. This could be created with a separate *Extruded Cut* or *Hole* feature. But in order to make that hole part of the *Revolved* feature, you need to sketch the axis of revolution so that it leaves a space between the profile and the axis.

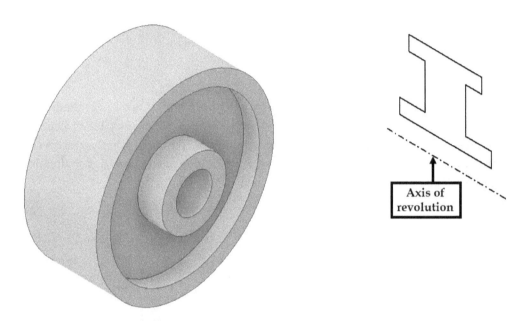

After completing the sketch, activate the **Revolve** command (On the ribbon, click **3D Model > Create > Revolve**); the sketch profile is selected, automatically. Click on the sketch to define the section of the *Revolved* feature, if the sketch is not already selected. Also, notice that the axis of revolution is selected automatically, if you have sketched the axis using the **Centerline** command. You need to click the **Axis** button on the dialog and select the axis if you have created it using the simple **Line** or **Construction** command.

On the **Revolve** dialog, select **Full** from the **Extents** drop-down; the sketch will be revolved by full 360 degrees. If you select **Angle** from the **Extents** drop-down, you need to type-in a value in the **Angle1** box. In addition to that, you need to specify the revolution direction using the direction options: **Direction 1** , **Direction 2** , **Symmetric** , and **Assymetric** . On the dialog, click **OK** to complete the *Revolved* feature.

Project Geometry

This command projects the edges of a 3D geometry onto a sketch plane. Activate the Sketch environment by selecting a plane or model face. On the **Sketch** tab of the ribbon, click **Create** panel > **Project** drop-down > **Project Geometry**. Click on the edges of the model geometry to project them on to the sketch plane. Press Esc to deactivate the command.

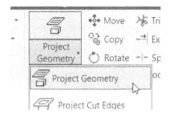

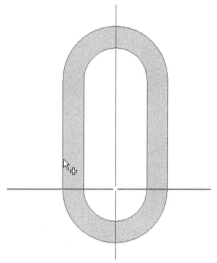

The projected element will be yellow in color and fully constrained. If you want to convert it into a normal sketch element, then right click on it and select **Break Link**.

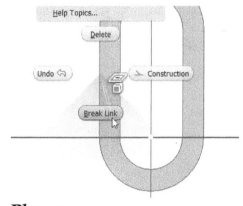

Planes

Each time you start a new part file, Inventor automatically creates default work planes. Planes are a specific type of elements in Inventor, known as Work Features. These features act as supports to your 3D geometry. In addition to the default work features, you can create your own additional planes. Until now, you have learned to create sketches on any of the default planes (XY, YZ, and XZ planes). If you want to create sketches and geometry at locations other than default planes, you can create new work planes manually. You can do this by using the commands available on the **Plane** drop-down of the **Work Features** panel.

Offset from Plane

This command creates a plane, which will be parallel to a face or another plane. Activate the **Offset from Plane** command (click **3D Model > Work Features > Plane** drop-down **> Offset from Plane** on the ribbon). Click on a flat face and drag the arrow that appears on the plane (or) type-in a value in the **Distance** box on the **Mini toolbar**.

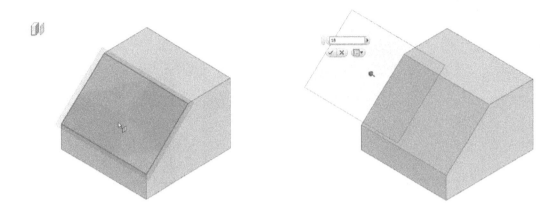

Click **OK** on the **Mini toolbar** to create the offset from plane.

Parallel to Plane through Point

This command creates a plane, which will be parallel to a selected point, face or plane through a point. Activate the **Parallel to Plane through Point** command (click **3D Model > Work Features > Plane** drop-down **> Parallel to Plane through Point** on the ribbon) and Select a planar face or work plane. Next, select a point on the part geometry.

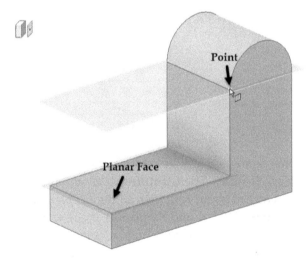

Midplane between Two Planes

This command creates a plane, which lies at the midpoint between two selected planes. You can also create a plane passing through the intersection point of the two selected faces. Activate the **Midplane between Two Planes** command (click **3D Model > Work Features > Plane** drop-down **> Midplane between Two Planes** on the ribbon) and click on two faces of the model geometry. Click **OK** to create the Midplane.

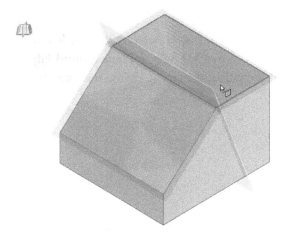 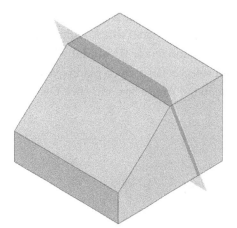

Another example of Midplane Between Two Planes.

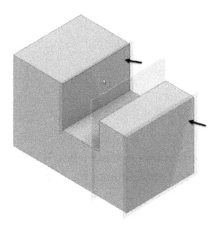

Midplane of Torus

This command creates a plane through the midplane of a torus. Activate the **Midplane of Torus** command (click **3D Model > Work Features > Plane** drop-down **> Midplane of Torus** on the ribbon) and select a torus to create the midplane.

Angle to Plane around Edge

This command creates a plane, which will be positioned at an angle to a face or plane. Activate the **Angle to Plane around Edge** command (click **3D Model > Work Features > Plane** drop-down **> Angle to Plane around Edge** on the ribbon) and select a flat face or plane. Next, click on an edge of the part geometry to define the rotation axis. Type-in a value in the **Angle** box and click **OK** to create the plane.

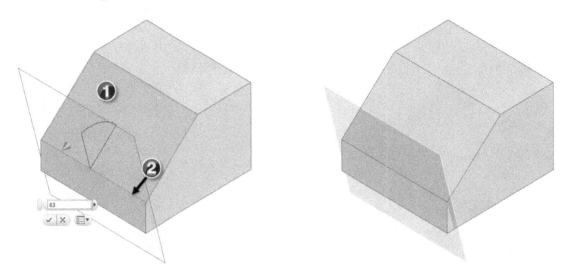

Three Points

This command creates a plane passing through three points. Activate the **Three Points** command (click **3D Model > Work Features > Plane** drop-down **> Three Points** on the ribbon) and select three points from the model geometry. A plane will be placed passing through these points.

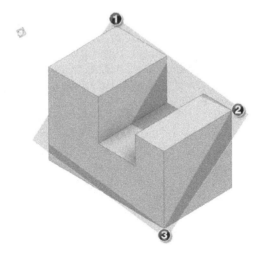

Two Coplanar Edges

This command creates a plane passing through two coplanar axes, edges or lines. Activate the **Two Coplanar Edges** command (click **3D Model > Work Features > Plane** drop-down **> Two Coplanar Edges** on the ribbon) and select two coplanar axes or edges or lines.

Extrude and Revolve Features

Coplanar Lines

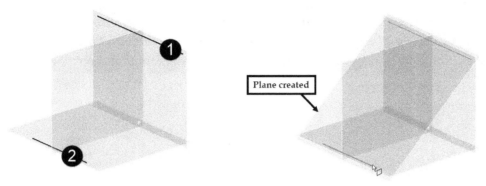

Coplanar Edges

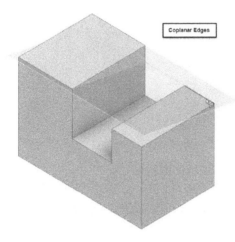

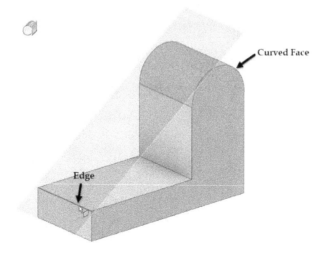 Tangent to Surface through Edge

This command creates a plane tangent to a curved face and passing through an edge. Activate this command (click **3D Model > Work Features > Plane** drop-down **> Tangent to Surface through Edge** on the ribbon) and select a curved face and a linear edge. A plane tangent to the selected face and passing through the edge appears.

Tangent to Surface through Point

This command creates a plane passing through a point and tangent to a curved face. Activate this command (click **3D Model > Work Features > Plane** drop-down **> Tangent to Surface through Point** on the ribbon) and select a curved face and a point. A plane tangent to the curved face and passing through a point will be created.

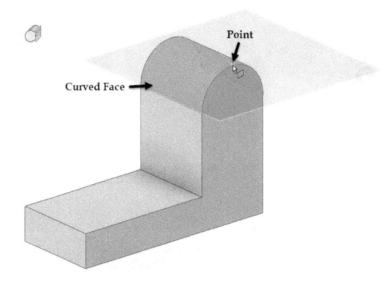

Tangent to Surface and Parallel to Plane

This command creates a plane, which is tangent to a curved face and parallel to a plane. Activate this command (click **3D Model > Work Features > Plane** drop-down **> Tangent to Surface and Parallel to Plane** on the ribbon) and select a curved face. Next, select a planar face or a plane; a plane tangent to the selected curved face and parallel to the plane appears.

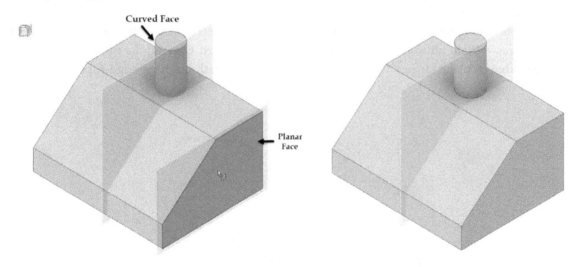

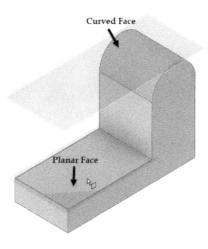

Normal to Axis through Point

This command creates a plane, which will be normal to an axis or edge and at a point. Activate this command (click **3D Model > Work Features > Plane** drop-down > **Normal to Axis through Point** on the ribbon) and select an axis or edge. Next, click on a point to define the location of the plane.

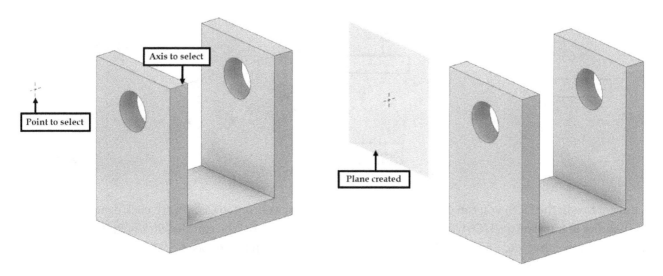

Normal to Curve at a Point

This command creates a plane, which will be normal to a line, curve, or edge. Activate this command by clicking **3D Model > Work Features > Plane** drop-down > **Normal to Curve at a Point** on the ribbon. Select an edge, line, curve, arc, or circle. Next, pick a point to define the location of the plane.

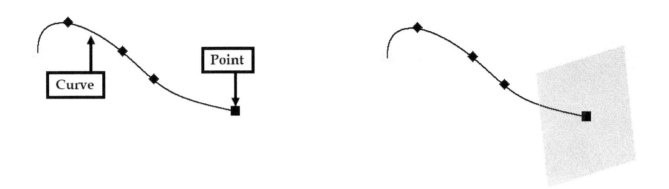

⌐ UCS

This command creates a new coordinate system in addition to the default one. Activate this command (click **3D Model > Work Features > UCS** on the ribbon). The UCS triad appears on the graphics window. Pick a point to specify the origin of the UCS. Next, select the point to specify the X-axis of the UCS. Select another point to specify the Y-axis; the UCS will be created.

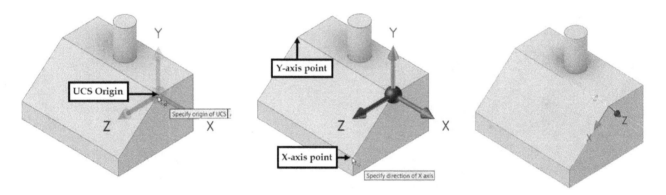

If you want to edit the UCS, you can double-click on anyone of the axes of the UCS. Next, click drag the X, Y, or Z arrow handles to translate the UCS triad along X, Y, or Z-axis, respectively. You can also click on the arrow handles, type-in a distance value, and then press Enter; the UCS will be moved up to the specified distance the selected axis.

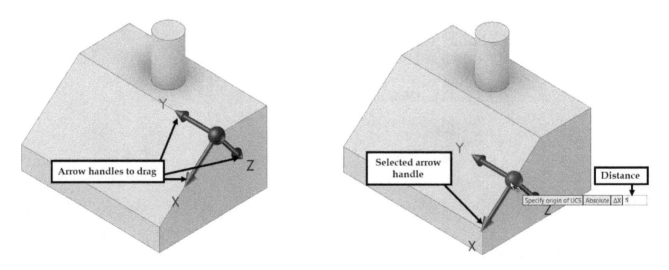

If you want to change the orientation of the UCS, you can rotate it about anyone of the axes. To do this, click on the shaft portion of an axis. Next, press and hold the left mouse button and drag the pointer; the UCS is rotated about the selected axis. You can also click on the shaft portion of the axis, and then specify the angle in the angle box.

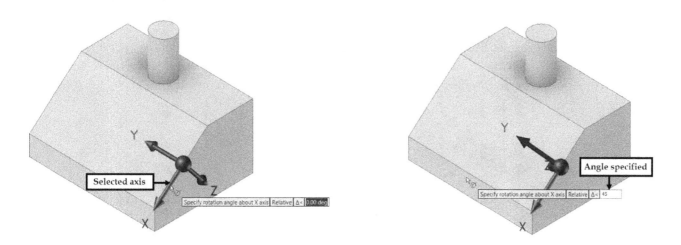

Additional options of the Extrude command

The **Extrude** command has some additional options to create complex features of a 3D geometry.

Operation

When you extrude a sketch, the **Operation** options determine whether the material is added, subtracted or intersected from an existing solid body.

Join

This option adds material to the geometry.

Cut

This option removes material from the geometry.

Intersect

This option creates a solid body containing the volume shared by two separate bodies.

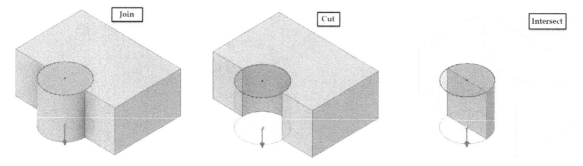

New Solid

This option creates a separate solid body. This will be helpful while creating multi-body parts.

Extents

On the **Extrude** dialog, the **Extents** section has various options to define the start and end limits of the *Extrude* feature. These options are **Distance**, **To Next**, **To, Between, All,** and **Distance from face**.

The **Distance** option extrudes the sketch up to the specified distance. On the **Extrude** dialog, select **Distance** from the **Extents** section. Specify the distance in the distance box and click on the required direction icon. There are four types of direction icons: *Direction 1, Direction 2, Symmetric* and *Asymmetric* icons.

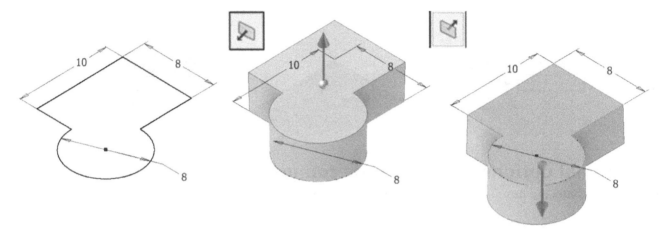

When you select the **Asymmetric** icon, you must specify the two distances in the **Distance1** and **Distance2** boxes, respectively.

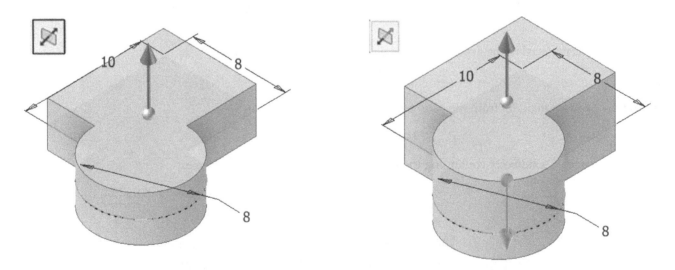

The **To Next** option extrudes the sketch through the face next to the sketch plane.

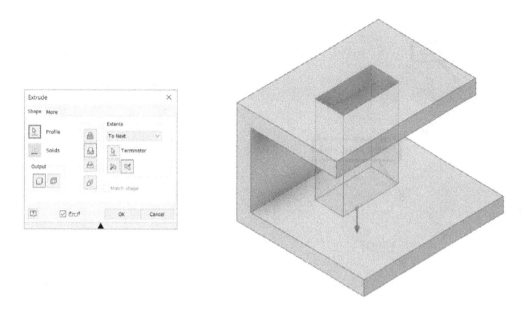

The **To** option extrudes the sketch up to a selected face. Ensure that the sketch will lie on the selected face, if projected. On the **Extrude** dialog, click on the **Join** icon to add material to the part and select **To** from the **Extents** section. Next, select the face or plane; the sketch will be extruded up to the selected face or plane.

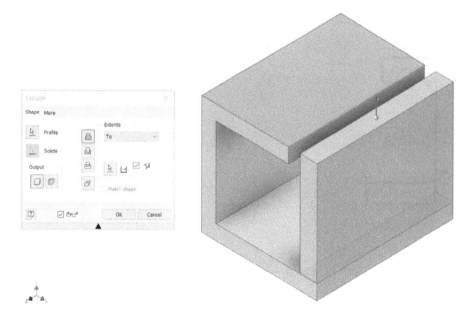

The **Between** option extrudes the sketch between the two selected faces. On the **Extrude** dialog, select **Between** from the **Extents** section, and then select two faces or planes; the sketch is extruded between the two faces.

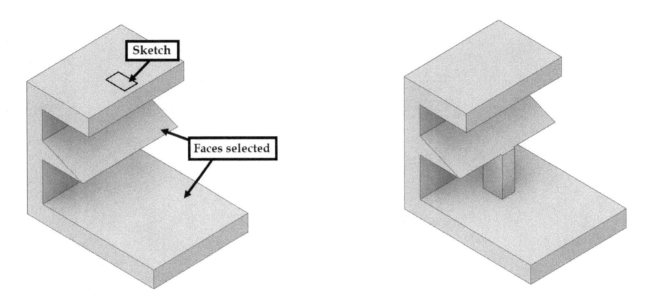

The **Distance from Face** option extrudes the sketch from the selected face up to the specified distance. On the **Extrude** dialog, select **Distance from Face** from the **Extents** section. Click on the selection button (Select surface to start the feature creation) displayed below the **Extents** drop-down and select the starting face. Next, specify the distance in the **Distance1** box. Click on anyone of the direction icons to specify the direction.

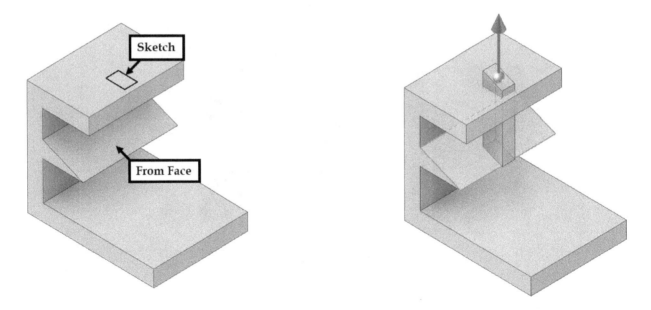

The **All** option extrudes the sketch throughout the 3D geometry. On the **Extrude** dialog, select **All** from the **Extents** section. Click on anyone of the direction icons to specify the direction.

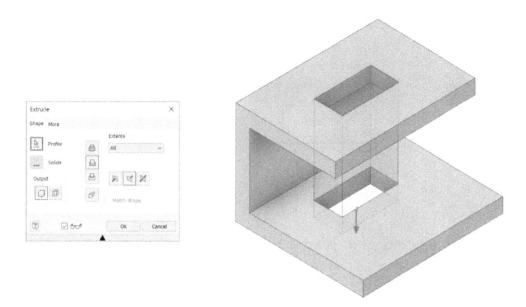

Match Shape

This option adds an *Extrude* feature to an existing feature using an open profile. It extends the profile to meet the adjacent edges. Activate the **Extrude** command, and then click on the open profile. On the dialog, check the **Match Shape** option. Notice that a rectangle boundary appears enclosing the entire geometry. Click in a region of the rectangle to specify the material side. Next, select the **Operation** and **Extent** type. Click **OK** to create the extruded feature.

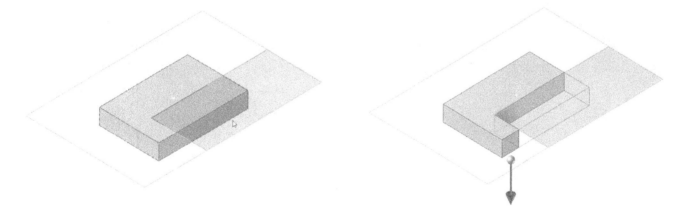

Adding Taper to the Extruded Feature

The **Taper** option will help you to apply draft to the extrusion. On the **Extrude** dialog, click the **More** tab and enter the angle value in the **Taper** box. You can apply the taper along the four directions: *Direction1, Direction2, Symmetric* and *Asymmetric*.

After specifying the draft angle, click on **Shape** tab and click on anyone of the direction icons under the **Extents** section.

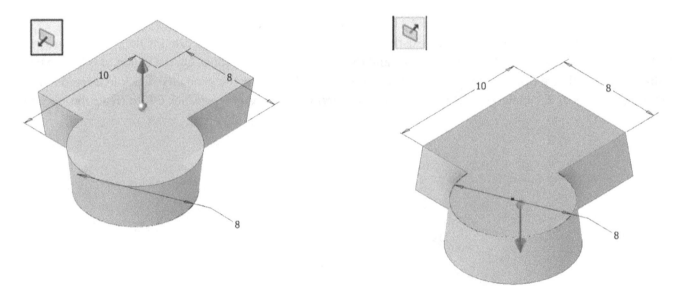

The draft angle can be changed dynamically using the arrow that appears on the geometry. A positive angle applies an inward draft and a negative angle applies an outward draft.

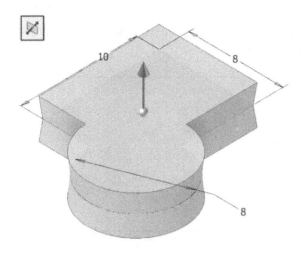 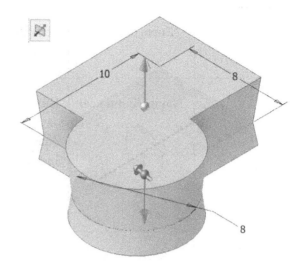

Click **OK** to complete the Extruded Feature.

View Modification commands

The model display in the graphics window can be changed using various view modification commands. Most of these commands are located on the **View** tab on the ribbon. These commands can also be accessed from Navigation bar in the graphics window. The following are some of the main view modification commands:

	Zoom All	The model will be fitted in the current size of the graphics window so that it will be visible completely.
	Pan	Activate this command, press and hold the left mouse button, and then drag the pointer to move the model view on the plane parallel to screen.
	Orbit	Activate this command and press and hold the left mouse button. Drag the pointer to rotate the model view.
	Zoom	Activate this command and press the left mouse button. Drag the mouse to vary the size of the objects accordingly.
	Look At	This command positions a selected planar face parallel to the screen. You can also select an edge to make is horizontal to the screen.
	Zoom window	Activate this command and drag a rectangle. The contents inside the rectangle will be zoomed.

	Zoom Selected	Activate this command and specify a point of the model; the view is zoomed in at the selected point.	
	Navigation wheel	This wheel has various navigation options such as **Zoom, Pan, Orbit, Rewind,** and so on.	
	Shaded with Edges	This represents the model with shades along with visible edges.	
	Shaded	This represents the model with shades without visible edges.	
	Wireframe	This represents the model in wireframe along with the hidden edges	

⌐	**Wireframe with hidden edges**	This represents the model in wireframe. The hidden edges are displayed in dashed lines.	
⌐	**Wireframe with Visible edges only**	This represents the model in wireframe. The hidden edges are not shown.	

Examples

Example 1 (Millimeters)

In this example, you will create the part shown below.

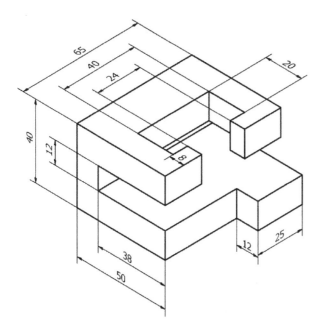

Creating the Base Feature

1. Start **Autodesk Inventor 2019** by double-clicking the **Autodesk Inventor 2019** icon on your desktop.
2. To start a new part file, click **Get Started > Launch > New** on the ribbon.

3. On the **Create New File** dialog, click the **Metric** folder under **Templates**.
4. Click the **Standard(mm).ipt** icon under the **Part – Create 2D and 3D Objects** section.
5. Click the **Create** button on the **Create New File** dialog.
6. To start a sketch, click **3D Model > Sketch > Start 2D Sketch** on the ribbon. Click on the XY plane. The sketch starts.

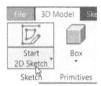

7. Click **Sketch > Create > Rectangle Two Point** on the ribbon. Click the origin point to define the first corner of the rectangle. Next, move the pointer toward top right corner and click to define the second corner.
8. Click **Sketch > Constrain > Dimension** on the ribbon.
9. Select the horizontal line of the rectangle, move the pointer upward, and then click.
10. Type 50 in the **Edit Dimension** box and click the green check ☑.
11. Select the vertical line of the rectangle, move the pointer horizontally, and then click to position the dimension.
12. Type 40 in the **Edit Dimension** box and click the green check ☑.
13. Press **Esc** to deactivate the **Dimension** command.

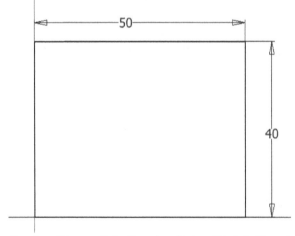

14. On the ribbon, click **Sketch > Exit > Finish Sketch**.
15. Click on the **Home** icon located at the top left corner of the ViewCube.

16. On the ribbon, click **3D Model > Create > Extrude**; the sketch is selected automatically.
17. On the **Extrude** dialog, under the **Extents** section select **Distance** from the drop-down.
18. Type-in **65** in the **Distance** box and click the **Symmetric** ☒ icon.
19. Click **OK** on the **Extrude** dialog to complete the *Extrude* feature.

Extrude and Revolve Features

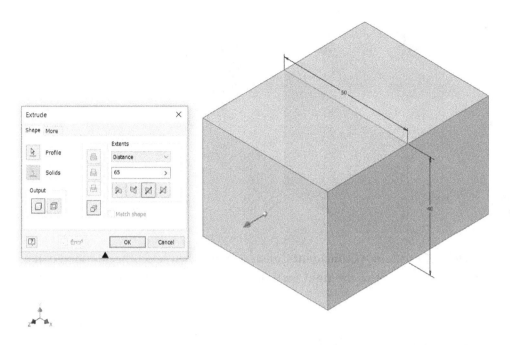

Creating the Extrude Cut throughout the Part model

1. To start a sketch, click **3D Model > Sketch > Start 2D Sketch** on the ribbon.
2. Click on the front face of the part geometry.

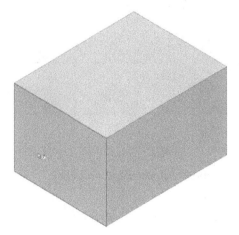

3. Click **Sketch > Create > Rectangle Two Point** on the ribbon.
4. Click near the upper portion of the right vertical edge.
5. Move the pointer diagonally toward bottom-left corner, and then click.

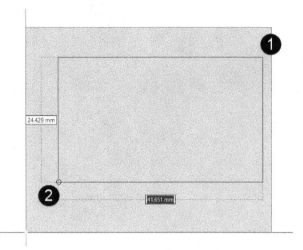

6. On the ribbon, click **Sketch > Constrain > Coincident Constraint**, and then select the midpoint of the right vertical line. Next, select the midpoint of the right vertical edge of the model; the two points are made coincident to each other.

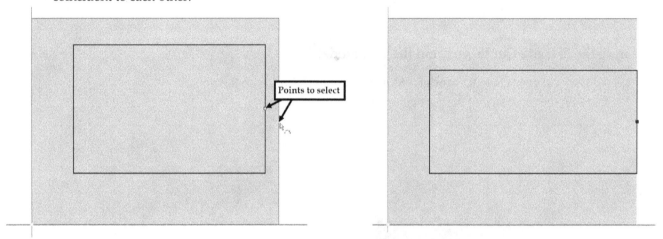

7. On the ribbon, click **Sketch> Constrain > Dimension**.
8. Select the horizontal line of the sketch, move the pointer vertically downward and click.
9. Type **38** in the **Edit Dimension** box and click the green check ✓.
10. Select the vertical line of the sketch, move the pointer horizontally and click to position the dimension.
11. Type **12** in the **Edit Dimension** box and click the green check ✓.
12. Press **Esc** to deactivate the **Dimension** command.
13. Click **Sketch > Exit > Finish Sketch** on the ribbon.
14. On the ribbon, click **3D Model > Create > Extrude**. On the **Extrude** dialog, click the **Cut** icon.
15. Next, select **All** from the **Extents** section.

Extrude and Revolve Features

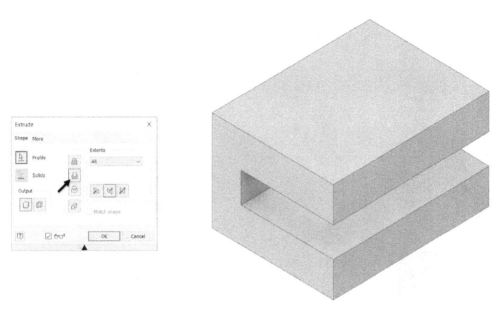

16. Click **OK** to create the cut throughout the part model.

Creating the Extruded Cut up to the surface next to the sketch plane

1. Click **3D Model > Sketch > Start 2D Sketch** on the ribbon and click on the top face of the part model, as shown.

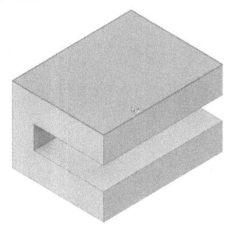

2. Activate the **Line** command (**Sketch > Create > Line** on the ribbon).
3. Click on the lower right portion of the model face to define the start point of the line. Move the pointer vertically upward and click.
4. Move the pointer horizontally toward left and type 8 in the length box attached to the pointer. Press Enter to create a horizontal line with a dimension.

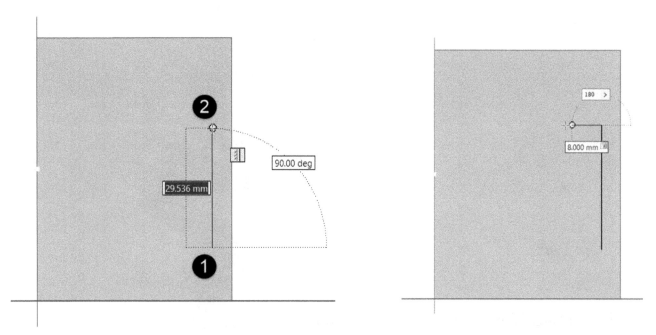

5. Move the pointer vertically upward and click. Move the pointer horizontally toward left, type 20 and press Enter. Move the pointer toward down and click.

6. Likewise, create the remaining three lines, as shown. Press **Esc** to deactivate the Line command.

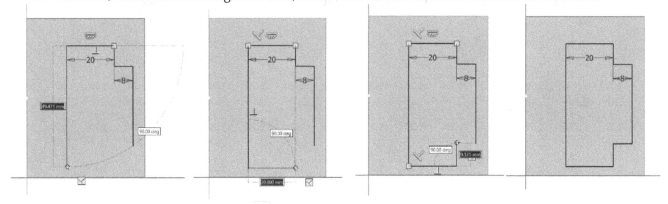

7. Click **Sketch > Constrain > Equal** on the ribbon.

8. Select the two vertical lines, as shown.

9. Select the two horizontal lines, as shown

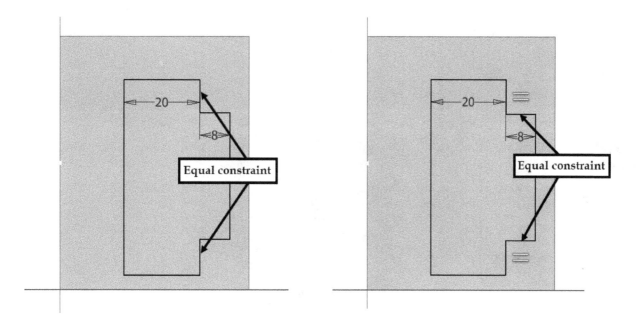

10. On the ribbon, click **Sketch > Constrain > Coincident Constraint**.
11. Select the midpoints of the right vertical line and right vertical edge; the selected points are made coincident to each other.
12. On the ribbon, click **Sketch > Constrain > Dimension**. Select the right vertical line of the sketch, move the pointer towards right and click. Type 24 in the **Edit Dimension** box and press Enter.
13. Likewise, apply the other dimensions as shown. Press **Esc** to deactivate the **Dimension** command.

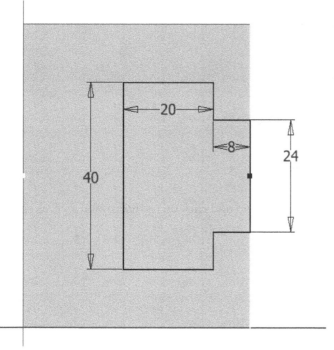

14. On the ribbon, click **Sketch > Exit > Finish Sketch**.
15. Click **3D Model > Create > Extrude** on the ribbon.
16. On the **Extrude** dialog, click the **Cut** icon and select **To Next** from the **Extents** drop-down as shown.

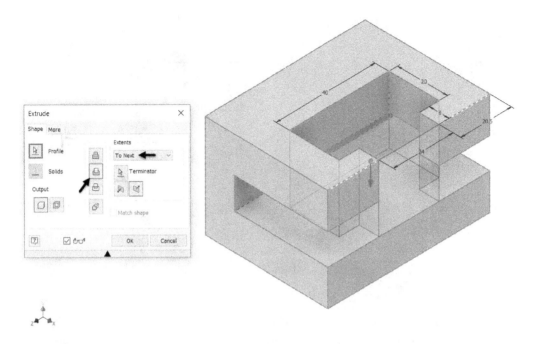

17. Click **OK** to create the *Extruded Cut* feature up to the surface next to the sketch plane.

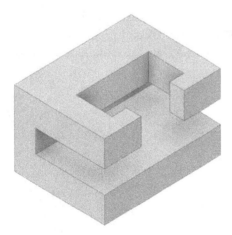

Extruding the sketch up to a Surface

1. Click **3D Model > Sketch > Start 2D Sketch** command and click on the horizontal face, as shown.

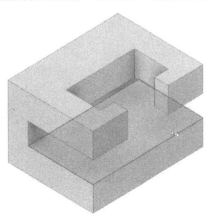

2. Draw a rectangle. Apply the coincident constraint between the top left corner of the rectangle and the top right corner of the model. Add dimensions and finish the sketch.

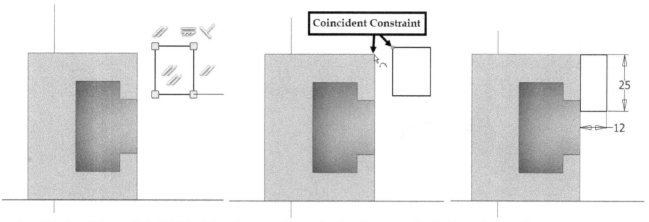

3. On the ribbon, click **3D Model > Create > Extrude**. On the **Extrude** dialog, select **To** from the **Extents** drop-down.
4. Select the bottom face of the part model, as shown.

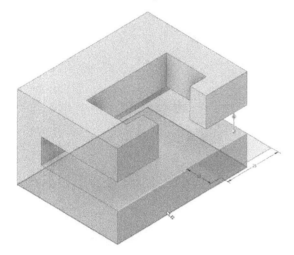

5. Make sure that the **Select to terminate feature by extending the face** option is checked.

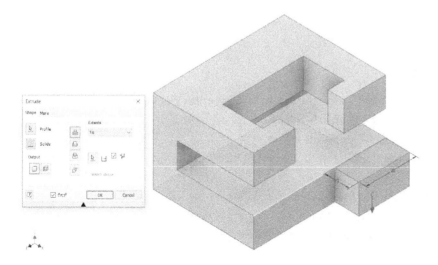

6. Click **OK** to complete the part model.

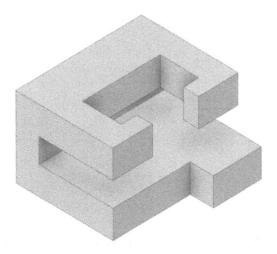

7. Save and close the file.

Example 2 (Inches)

In this example, you will create the part shown below.

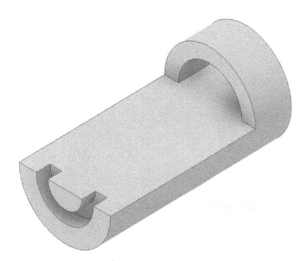

Creating the Revolved Solid Feature

1. Start **Autodesk Inventor 2019** by double-clicking the **Autodesk Inventor 2019** icon on your desktop.
2. To start a new part file, click **Get Started > Launch > New** on the ribbon.
3. On the **Create New File** dialog, click the **Templates** folder.
4. Click the **Standard.ipt** icon under the **Part – Create 2D and 3D Objects** section. Click **Create** to start new part file.
5. On the ribbon, click **3D Model > Sketch > Start 2D Sketch**. Click on the **XZ** plane.
6. On the ribbon, click **Sketch > Create > Rectangle > Rectangle Three Point Center** and specify the three points of the rectangle, as shown. Press **Esc** to deactivate the Rectangle command.

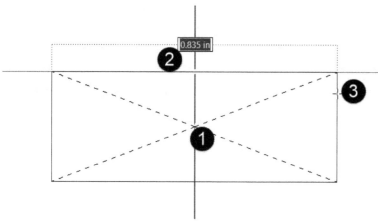

7. Click **Sketch > Constrain > Dimension** on the ribbon and apply dimensions, as shown.
8. On the ribbon, click **Sketch > Constrain > Coincident Constraint**, and then select the midpoint of the top horizontal line. Next, select the sketch origin.

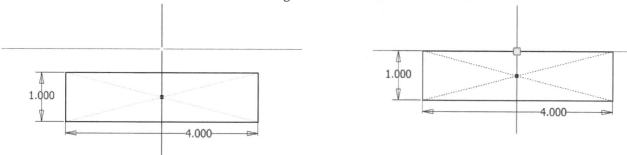

9. Click **Sketch > Exit > Finish Sketch** on the ribbon.
10. Click the **Home** icon located at the top left corner of the ViewCube.

11. Activate the **Revolve** command (click **3D Model > Create > Revolve** on the ribbon); the sketch profile is selected, automatically.
12. On the **Revolve** dialog, click **Axis** selection button and select the axis line, as shown.
13. Select the **Angle** option from the **Extents** drop-down and enter **180** in the **Angle1** box.
14. Click the **Direction1** icon and click **OK** to create the *Revolve* feature.

Extrude and Revolve Features

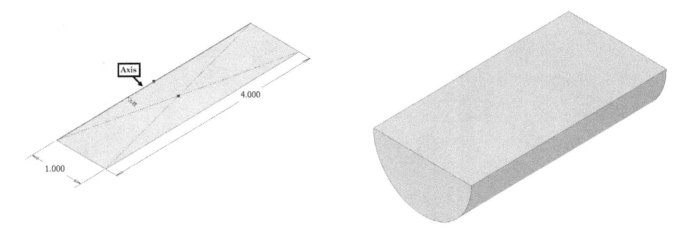

Creating the Revolved Cut

1. On the ribbon, click **3D Model > Sketch > Start 2D Sketch**. Click on the top face of the part model, as shown.

2. Draw the sketch and apply the dimensions, as shown.

3. On the ribbon, click **Sketch > Constrain > Collinear Constraint** and select the left vertical line of the sketch. Next, select the left vertical edge of the model. Click **Finish Sketch**.

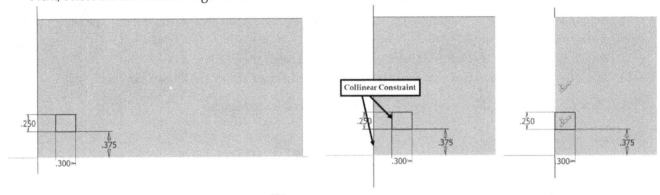

4. Click **3D Model > Work Features > Axis** on the ribbon. Next, click the curved face of the *Revolved* feature.

5. Activate the **Revolve** command and click in the region of the sketch.

6. On the **Revolve** dialog, click the **Axis** selection button and select the newly created axis from the **Model** tab of the Browser window.

Extrude and Revolve Features

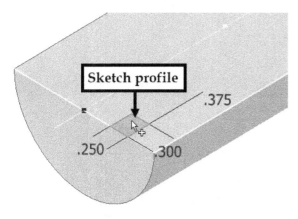

7. Click the **Cut** icon on the **Revolve** dialog.

8. Select the **To Next** option from the **Extents** drop-down. Click the **Direction1** 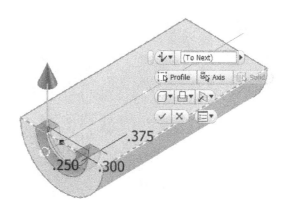icon and click **OK** to create the *Revolved Cut* feature.

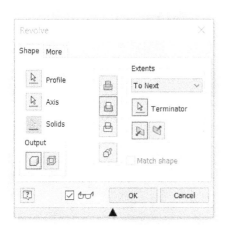

Adding a Revolved Feature to the model

1. Activate the **Create 2D Sketch** command and click on the top face of the part model.
2. Draw the sketch and apply dimensions and constraint, as shown. Finish the sketch.

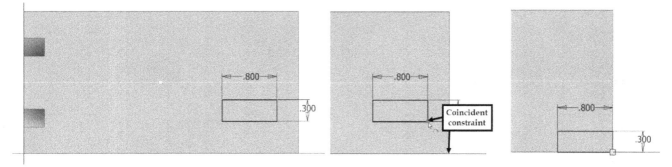

3. Activate the **Revolve** command and select the sketch from the part model.
4. On the **Revolve** dialog, click the **Axis** selection button and select the axis, as shown. Make sure that the **Join** icon is selected.
5. Select the **To** option from the **Extents** drop-down and select the top face of the model geometry.

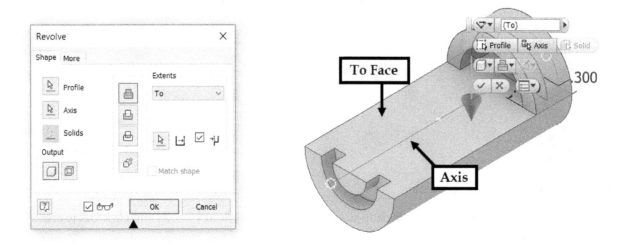

6. Click **OK** to add the *Revolved* feature to the part model.

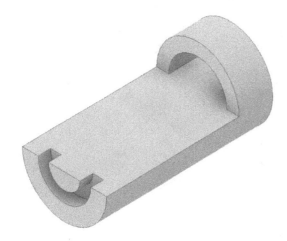

7. Save and close the file.

Questions

1. How to create parallel planes in Inventor?
2. What are the **Direction** options available on the **Extrude** dialog?
3. List the **Extents** types available on the **Extrude** dialog.
4. How do you extrude an open profile in Inventor?
5. List the operations available on the **Extrude** dialog.
6. How to create angled planes in Inventor?

Exercises
Exercise 1 (Inches)

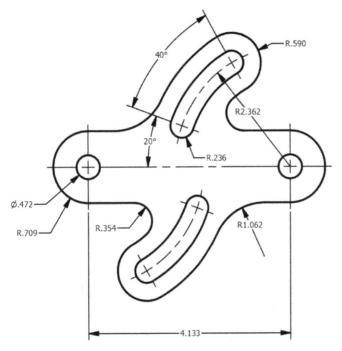

Exercise 2 (Millimetres)

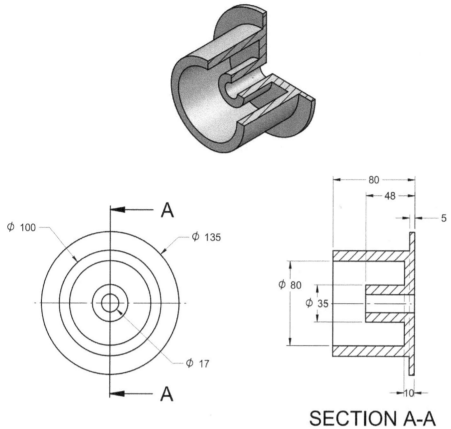

ϕ 100

ϕ 135

ϕ 17

80

48

5

ϕ 80

ϕ 35

10

SECTION A-A

Exercise 3 (Inches)

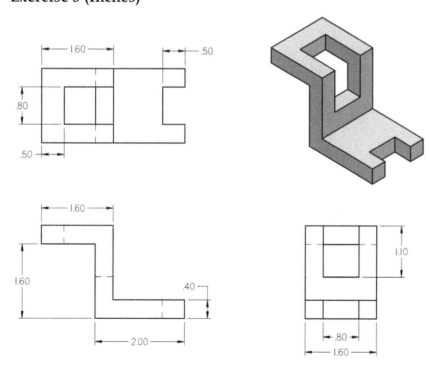

1.60

.50

.80

.50

1.60

1.60

.40

2.00

1.10

.80

1.60

115

Exercise 4 (Millimetres)

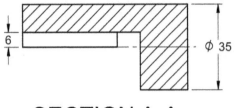

SECTION A-A

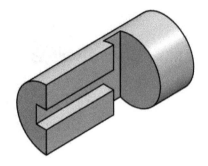

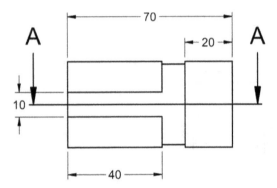

116

Chapter 4: Placed Features

So far, all of the features that were covered in previous chapter were based on two-dimensional sketches. However, there are certain features in Inventor that do not require a sketch at all. Features that do not require a sketch are called placed features. You can simply place them on your models. However, to do so, you must have some existing geometry. Unlike a sketch-based feature, you cannot use a placed feature for the first feature of a model. For example, to create a *Fillet* feature, you must have an already existing edge. In this chapter, you will learn how to add placed features to your design.

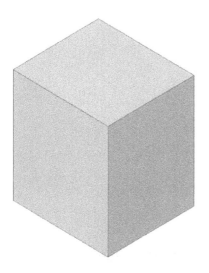
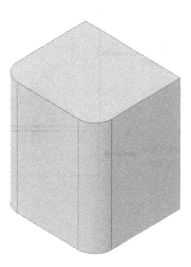

The topics covered in this chapter are:

- *Holes*
- *Threads*
- *Fillets*
- *Chamfers*
- *Drafts*
- *Shells*

Hole

As you know, it is possible to use the *Extrude* command to create cuts and remove material. But, if you want to drill holes that are of standard sizes, the **Hole** command is a better way to do this. The reason for this is it has many hole types already predefined for you. All you have to do is choose the correct hole type and size. The other benefit is when you are going to create a 2D drawing, Inventor can place the correct hole annotation, automatically. Activate this command (Click **3D Model > Modify > Hole** on the ribbon) and you will notice that the **Properties** panel appears on the screen. The components of the **Properties** panel are shown in the figure below. There are options in this panel that make it easy to create different types of holes.

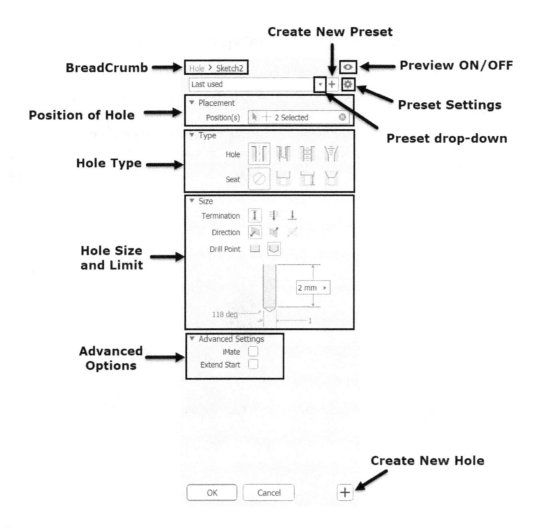

Simple Hole

To create a simple hole feature, select **Type > Simple Hole** on the **Properties** panel. Type-in a value in the **Diameter** box attached to the hole image in the **Size** section.

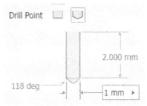

Next, select the **Termination** type. If you want a through hole, select **Termination > Through All**. If you want the hole only up to some depth, then select **Termination > Distance**, and then type-in a value in the **Hole Depth** box attached to the hole image.

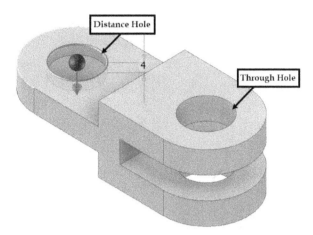

If you want the hole only up to a surface, then select **Termination > To** and select a face or surface on the graphics window; the hole will be created up to the selected surface.

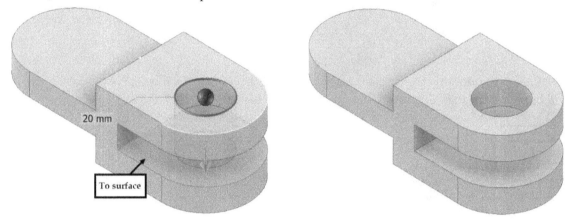

The **Drill Point** section has two options to define the depth of the hole: **Flat** and **Angle**. The **Flat** option creates a hole with a flat bottom. The **Angle** option creates a hole with an angled bottom. The **Drill Point Angle** box defines the angle of the cone tip at the bottom.

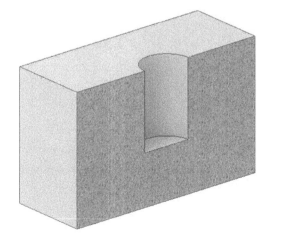

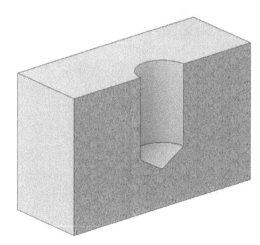

After specifying the settings on the **Properties** panel, click on a face to place the hole. Next, you need to specify the exact location of the hole by adding constraints or dimension or both. To do this, click the **Sketch** link in the Bread Crumbs of the **Properties** panel; the **Sketch** environment is activated. Add dimensions and constraints to define the hole position. You can also add multiple hole points by using the **Point** command (on the ribbon, click **Sketch > Create > Point**). Next, click the **Hole** link in the Bread Crumbs area of the **Properties** panel.

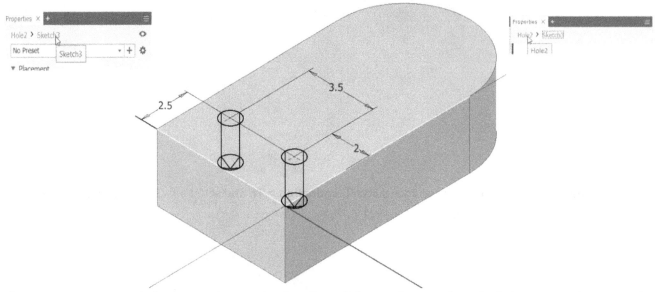

If you want to create a hole concentric to a circular edge, click on a face to place the hole. Next, select a circular edge; the hole will be concentric to it. Click **OK** to complete the hole feature.

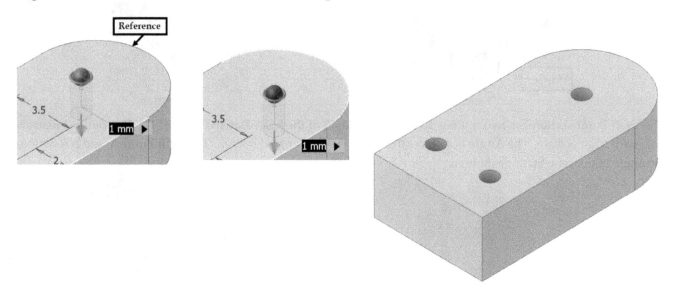

Extend Start

The **Extend Start** option is available in the **Advanced Settings** section and is used to extend the hole beyond its starting point. Select this option to remove any portion of the model geometry that blocks the starting point of the hole, as shown.

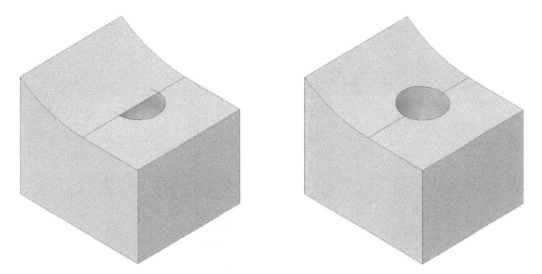

Saving the Hole Settings

While creating a hole, Inventor allows you to save the settings specified on the **Properties** panel for future use. You can use these settings to create a hole with same specifications multiple times. On the **Properties** panel, click the **Create new preset** icon next to the **Preset** drop-down. Next type a name for the preset and click the blue check; the settings are saved. You can access the saved settings from the **Preset** drop-down.

You can make changes to the pre-set settings and save it using the **Save Current** option available on the **Preset Settings** drop-down. Likewise, you can rename of delete the preset using the **Rename Current** and **Delete Current** options, respectively.

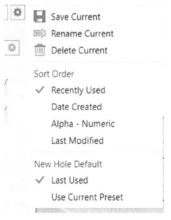

Counterbored Hole

A counterbore hole is a large diameter hole added at the opening of another hole. It is used to accommodate a fastener below the level of the workpiece surface. To create a counterbore hole, select **Type > Seat > Counterbored**. Next, specify the Counterbore Diameter, Counterbore Depth and Diameter. Specify the desired **Drill Point** option (**Flat** or **Angle**). If you click the **Flat** option, then you need to specify only the **Hole Depth** value. If you click the **Angle** option, then specify the **Hole Depth** and **Drill Point Angle** value.

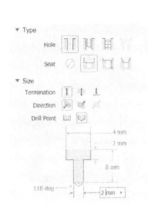
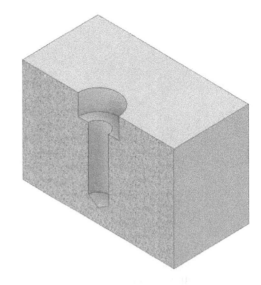

Countersink Hole

A countersink hole has an enlarged V-shaped opening to accommodate the fastener below the level of the work piece surface. To create a countersink hole, select **Type > Seat > Countersink**. Type-in values in the **Diameter**, **Countersink Diameter**, and **Countersink Angle** boxes. Set the hole depth and end condition.

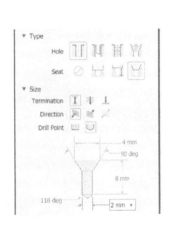
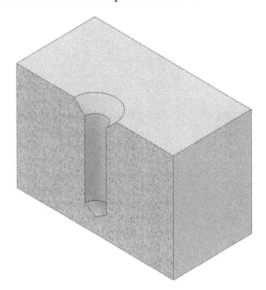

Tapped Hole

To create a tapped hole feature, select **Type > Hole > Tapped Hole**. Under the **Threads** section, select the thread standard from **Type** drop-down and also, select the **Size, Designation** and **Class**. Check the **Full Depth** option to create threads for the full depth of the hole. If you uncheck this option, you need to specify the thread depth in the **Thread Depth** box. Specify the desired thread direction from the **Thread** section. Specify the remaining hole options that are similar to the simple hole feature. Click **OK** to create the Tapped Hole.

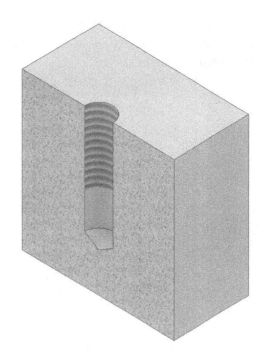

Taper Tapped Hole

Tapering is the process of decreasing the hole diameter toward one end. A tapered tapped hole has a thread and the diameter gradually becomes smaller towards the bottom. To create a tapered tapped hole, select **Type > Hole > Taper Tapped Hole**. Next, you need to specify the thread **Type** and **Size**. The tapered thread types and sizes are different from the normal threads. Next, you need to specify the thread **Direction** and thread depth. Click **OK** to create the Taper Tapped Hole.

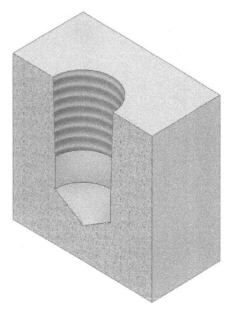

Thread

This command adds a thread feature to a cylindrical face. If you add a thread feature to a 3D geometry, Inventor can automatically place the correct thread annotation in the 2D drawing. Activate this command (click **3D Model > Modify > Thread** on the ribbon) and click the **Specification** tab on the **Thread** dialog. Next, specify the

Thread Type and click on a cylindrical face of the part geometry. The **Size** is automatically selected as per the size of the cylindrical face of the part geometry. Next, specify the **Designation** and **Class** values. Also, select the thread direction (**Right hand** or **Left hand**).

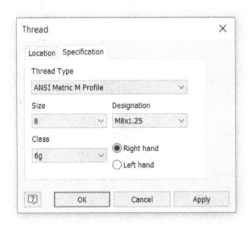
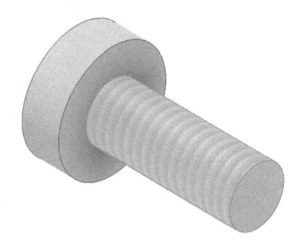

Click the **Location** tab on the dialog and notice that the **Full Length** option is selected by default. It creates the thread up to the entire length of the cylindrical face. Uncheck this option if you want to specify the length of the thread in the **Length** box. Next, enter a value in the **Offset** box, if you want to create thread at a distance from the start face of the cylinder.

Select the **Display in Model** option to view the thread in the part geometry. Note that if you deselect this option, the thread will not be displayed in the part geometry. But, you can view the thread in the 2D Drawing. Click **OK** to complete the thread feature.

Fillet

This command breaks the sharp edges of a model and blends them. You do not need a sketch to create a blend. All you need to have is model edges. To activate this command, click **3D Model > Modify > Fillet** on the ribbon. Click **Edge Fillet** on the top-left corner of the **Fillet** dialog and select the edges to fillet. As you start selecting edges, you will see a preview of the geometry. Inventor allows you to select the edges, which are located at the back of the model without rotating it. By mistake, if you have selected a wrong edge, you can deselect it by holding the Shift key and selecting the edge again. You can change the radius by typing a value in the **Radius** box displayed in the Mini toolbar. As you change the radius, all the selected edges will be updated. This is because they are all part of one instance. If you want the edges to have different radii, you must create blends in separate instances. Select the **Tangent Fillet** from the **Type** drop-down to create fillets which are tangent to the adjacent faces. Select the required number of edges and click **OK** to complete fillet feature. The *Fillet* feature will be listed in the **Model Window**.

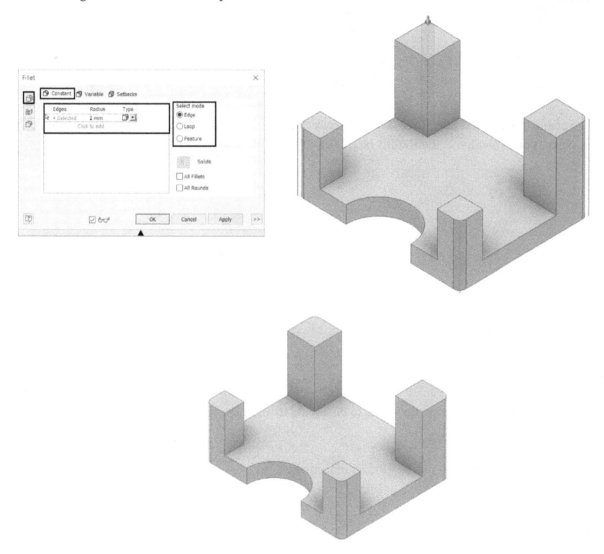

Smooth Fillet

By default, the edge fillets are tangent to the adjacent faces. However, if you want to create a smooth fillet that is curvature continuous with the adjacent faces, then select the **Smooth G2 Fillet** option from the **Type** drop-down on the **Fillet** dialog. Next, type-in a value in the **Radius** box.

Inverted Fillet

The **Inverted Fillet** option helps you to create convex or concave fillets. Convex fillets are created on exterior edges. Whereas, the concave fillets are created on interior edges.

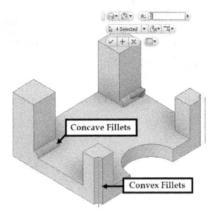

If you want to create the inverted fillet, then select the **Inverted Fillet** option from the **Type** drop-down on the **Fillet** dialog. Next, type-in a value in the **Radius** box. Click **OK** to create the inverted fillet.

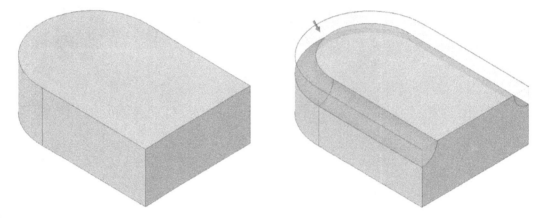

Selection Modes

The **Fillet** command allows you to select the edges to be filleted using three selection modes: **Edges**, **Loops**, and **Features**.

The **Edges** selection mode allows you to select individual edges.

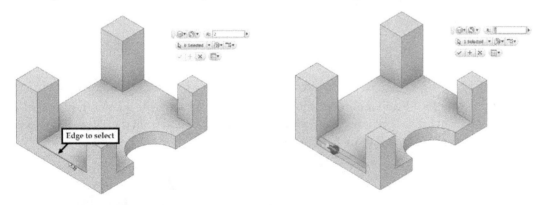

The **Loop** selection mode allows you to select a loop of edges.

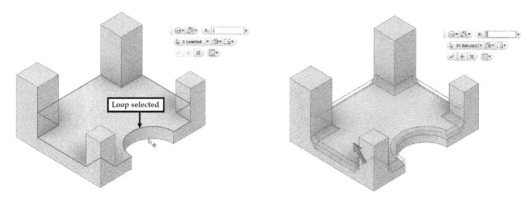

The **Features** selection mode allows you to select the entire feature to be filleted.

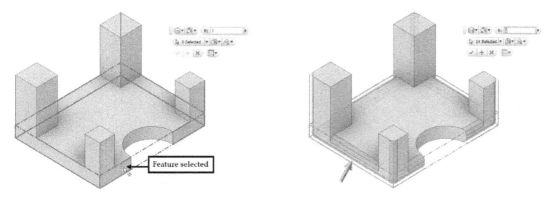

Solids

The **Fillet** command has options to create fillets or rounds without selecting the edges individually. These options are available in the **Solid** section of the **Fillet** dialog.

The **All Fillets** option creates fillets on the interior edges of the model, automatically.

The **All Rounds** option creates rounds on the exterior edges of the model, automatically.

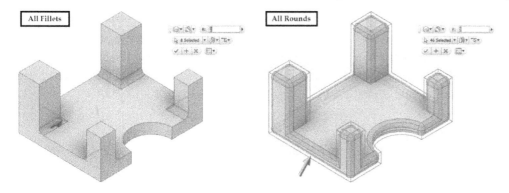

Variable Radius Fillet

Inventor allows you to create a fillet with a varying radius along the selected edge. Activate the **Fillet** command to create a variable fillet. On the **Fillet** dialog, click the **Variable** tab, and then click in the **Edges** section. Next, select the edge to add a fillet. Specify the variable radius points on the selected edge. Drag the arrows to change the radius value at each location. You can also change the radius values of each point in the **Fillet** dialog box. Check the **Smooth radius transition** option, if you want a smooth transition between the variable radius points. Click **OK** to create the variable radius fillet.

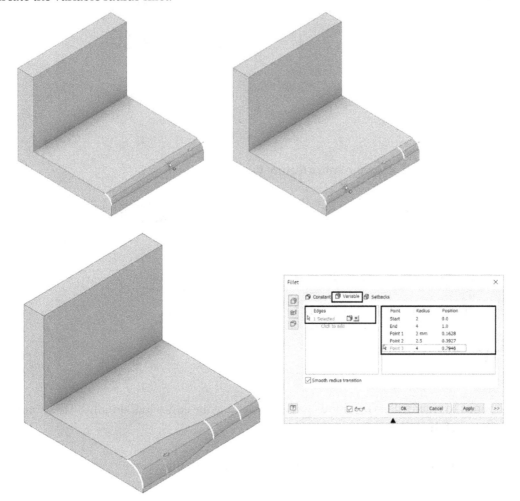

Corner Setback

If you create fillets on three edges that come together at a corner, you have the option to control how these three fillets are blended together. Activate the **Fillet** command and select the three edges that meet together at a corner. Next, click the **Setbacks** tab on the **Fillet** dialog, and then click on the vertex where the three fillets meet; the three edges and setback values appear on the dialog. Click in the **Setback** boxes of the individual edges, and then change their values. Check the **Minimal** option, if you do not want to apply the setback.

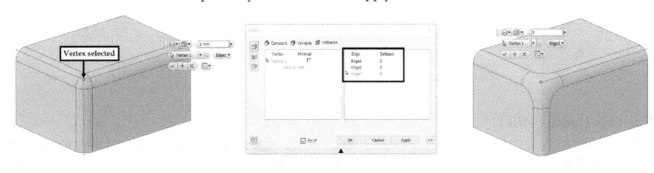

Face Fillet

This option creates a fillet between two faces. The faces are not required to be connected with each other. On the **Fillet** dialog, click the **Face Fillet** icon, and then click on two faces. Next, type-in a value in the **Radius** box and click **OK**.

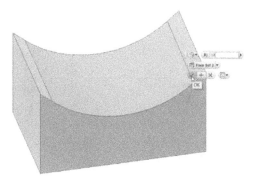

Full Round Fillet

This option creates a fillet between three faces. It replaces the middle face with a fillet. On the **Fillet** dialog, click the **Full Round Fillet** icon and click on three faces of the model geometry. Click **OK** to replace the middle face with a fillet.

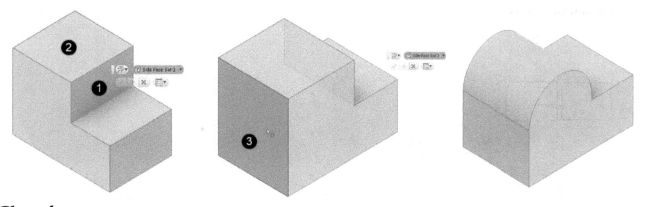

Chamfer

The **Chamfer** and **Fillet** commands are commonly used to break sharp edges. The difference is that the **Chamfer** command adds a bevelled face to the model. A chamfer is also a placed feature. Activate this command (click **3D Model > Modify > Chamfer** on ribbon) and click the **Distance** icon on the top left corner of the **Chamfer** dialog. Select the edge to chamfer and type-in a value in the **Distance** box. Click **OK** to complete the chamfer.

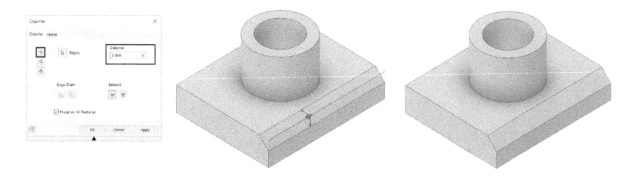

Distance and Angle chamfer

This option lets you to create a chamfer by defining its distance and angle values. On the **Chamfer** dialog, click the **Distance and Angle** icon. Select a face from the part geometry, and then select the edge that is coincident with it. Type-in values in the **Distance** and **Angle** boxes; the distance and angle values are measured from the selected face. Click **OK** to complete the feature.

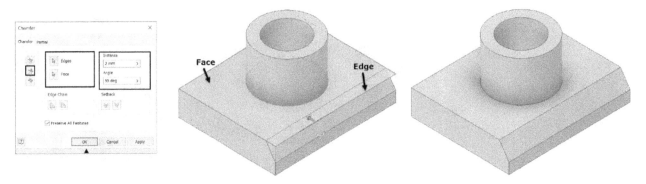

Two Distances chamfer

If you want a chamfer to have different setbacks on both sides of the edge, then click the **Two Distances** icon on the **Chamfer** dialog and click on the edge to chamfer. Type-in values in the **Distance 1** and **Distance 2** boxes on the dialog. If you want to switch the setback distance, then click the **Flip Distances** button on the dialog. Click **OK**.

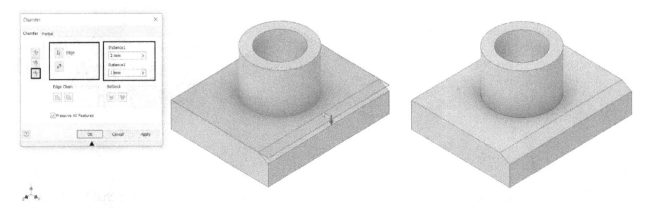

The Face Draft command

When creating cast or plastic parts, you are often required to add draft on them so that they can be molded easily. A draft is an angle or taper applied to the faces of components so that they can be removed from a mold easily. The following illustration shows a molded part with and without draft.

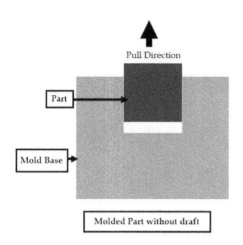

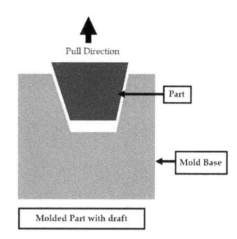

The **Face Draft** command will help you to apply draft to the model geometry. To activate this command, click **3D Model > Modify > Draft** on the ribbon. There are three draft options in the **Face Draft** dialog: **Fixed Edge**, **Fixed Plane** and **Parting Line**.

Fixed Edge

The **Fixed Edge** option uses an edge to define the pull direction of the draft. Click the **Fixed Edge** icon on the **Face Draft** dialog and select an edge from the model geometry; the pull direction is defined. Next, click on the **Faces to draft** selection button and select the faces to draft. Specify the angle in the **Draft Angle** box. To reverse the direction of the draft, click the **Flip Pull Direction** icon. Click **OK** to create the draft feature.

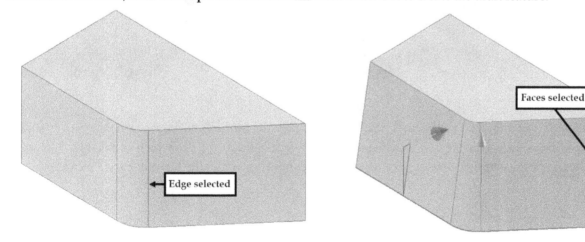

Fixed Plane

On the **Face Draft** dialog, click the **Fixed Plane** icon, and then select a face, which will act as a reference plane (fixed face) for the draft. The draft angle will be measured with reference to this face. After selecting the reference plane (fixed face), click the **Faces to Draft** selection button and select the faces to draft. Next, type-in a positive or negative value in the **Draft Angle** box. If you want to flip the draft direction, then click the **Flip Pull Direction** icon. Click **OK** to apply draft to the model.

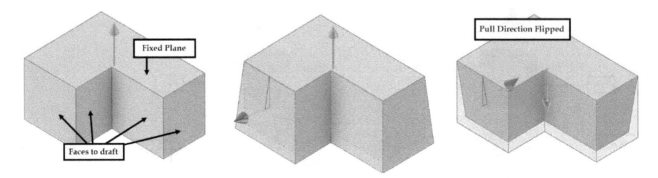

Shell

The **Shell** is another useful command that can be applied directly to a solid model. It allows you to take a solid geometry and make it hollow. This can be a powerful and timesaving technique, when designing parts that call for thin walls such as bottles, tanks, and containers. This command is easy to use. You should have a solid part to use this command. Activate this command from the **Modify** panel (On the ribbon, click **3D Model > Modify > Shell**) and select the faces to remove. Type-in the wall thickness in the **Thickness** box. Click the **Inside** , **Outside** , or **Both Sides** button to specify whether the thickness is added inside or outside or both sides of the model.

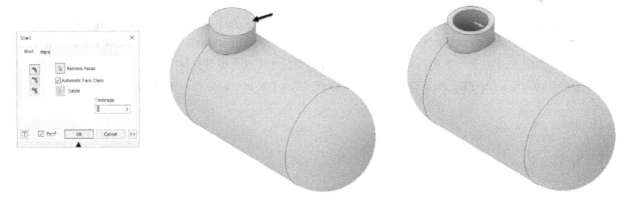

If you want to shell a portion with a different thickness value, click the **More** button section and click **Click to add** under the **Unique Face Thickness** section. Select the outer face of the portion to which you want a different thickness value. Type the alternate thickness value in the **Thickness** box under the **Unique Face Thickness** section.

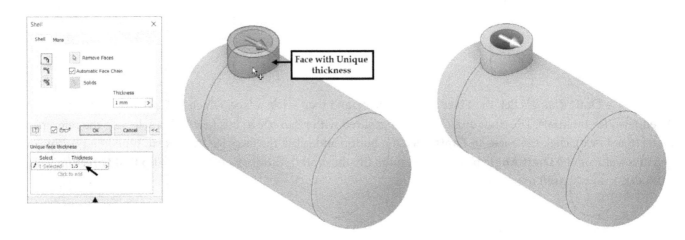

If you want to shell the solid body without removing any faces, then simply type-in a value in the **Thickness** box and click **OK**. This creates the shell without removing the faces. Change the **Visual style** to **Wireframe** or **Shaded with Hidden Edges** to view the shell.

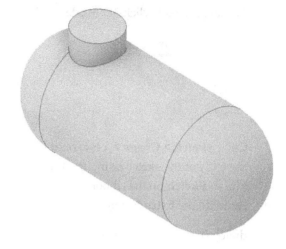

Examples

Example 1 (Millimeters)

In this example, you will create the part shown below.

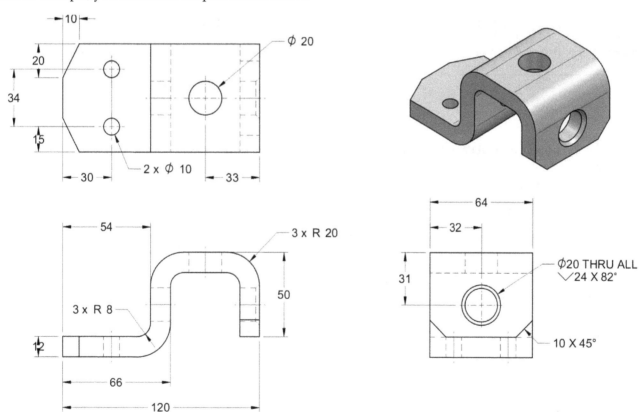

1. Start **Autodesk Inventor 2019** by double-clicking the **Autodesk Inventor 2019** icon on your desktop.
2. To start a new part file, click **Get Started > Launch > New** on the ribbon.

3. On the **Create New File** dialog, click the **Metric** folder under **Templates**.
4. Click the **Standard(mm).ipt** icon under the **Part – Create 2D and 3D Objects** section.
5. Click the **Create** button on the **Create New File** dialog.
6. To start a sketch, click **3D Model > Sketch > Start 2D Sketch** on the ribbon. Click on the **XY** plane.

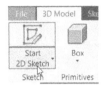

7. Click **Sketch > Create > Line**, on the ribbon. Draw a sketch and offset it up to 12 mm distance. Next, close the ends of the sketch using the **Line** command. Add dimensions to fully constrain the sketch. Click **Finish Sketch** on the ribbon.
8. Activate the **Extrude** command (on the ribbon, click **3D Model > Create > Extrude**). On the **Extrude** dialog, type 64 in the **Distance1** box and click the **Symmetric** icon. Click **OK**.

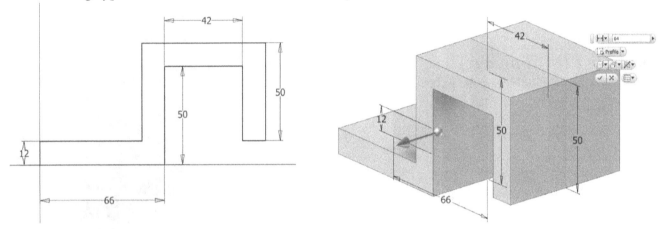

9. On the ribbon, click **3D Model > Modify > Hole**. Click on the right-side face of the part model, as shown.

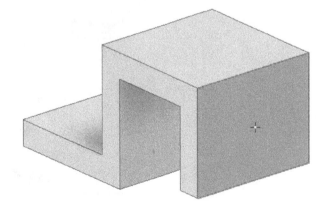

10. On the Properties panel, click **Type > Hole > Simple Hole**. Also, select **Type > Seat > Countersink**.

11. Under **Size** section, set the **Countersink Diameter** and **Countersink Angle** values to **24** and **82**, respectively. Set the **Diameter** value to **20 mm**. Also, select **Size > Termination > Through All**.

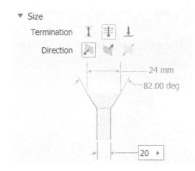

12. On the **Properties** panel, click the **Sketch2** link in the Breadcrunbs area; the Sketch environment is activated.

13. Add a dimension between the hole point and the top edge, as shown.

14. Click **Sketch > Constrain > Vertical Constraint** on the ribbon. Select the hole point and the midpoint of the top edge; the two points are vertically aligned.

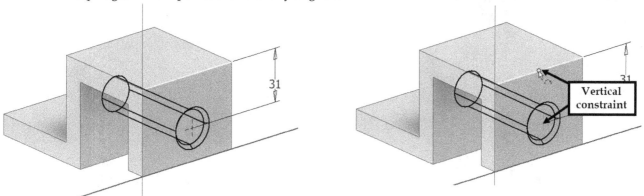

15. Click the **Hole** link on the **Properties** panel, and then click **OK** to complete the hole feature.

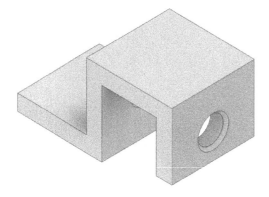

16. Activate the **Hole** command and click on the top face of the part model.
17. On the **Properties** panel, select **Preset drop-down > Last used**. Next, select **Type > Seat > None**.

18. On the **Properties** panel, click the **Sketch3** link in the Breadcrunbs area; the Sketch environment is activated.

19. On the ribbon, click **Sketch > Constrain > Horizontal Constraint** 〰. Select the center point of the hole and the midpoint of the right edge; the two points are aligned horizontally.

20. On the ribbon, click **Sketch > Constrain > Vertical Constraint** 🔏. Select the center point of the hole and the midpoint of the back edge; the two points are aligned vertically.

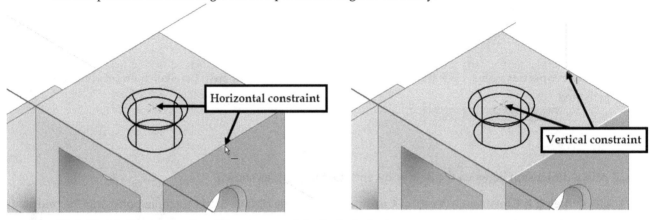

21. Click **Finish Sketch** on the ribbon to complete the hole feature.

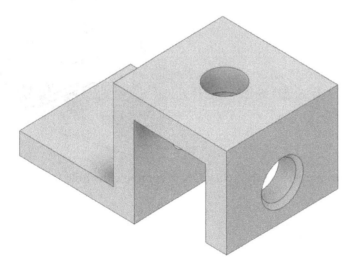

22. Click the top-left corner point of the ViewCube, as shown; this changes the view orientation of the part model.

23. Activate the **Create 2D Sketch** command and click on the lower top face of the part model. Place two points and add dimensions to define the hole location, as shown. Click **Finish Sketch** on the ribbon.

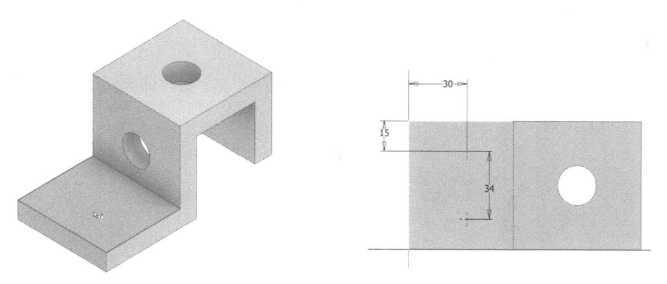

24. Click **3D Model > Modify > Hole** to activate the **Hole** command. On the **Properties** panel, select **Type > Hole > Simple Hole**. Set the **Diameter** value to 10mm.

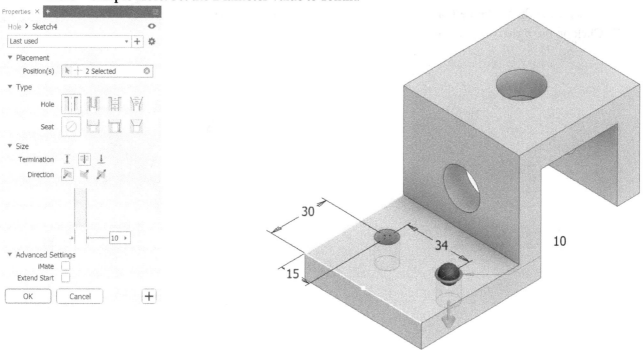

25. Click **OK** to complete the hole feature.

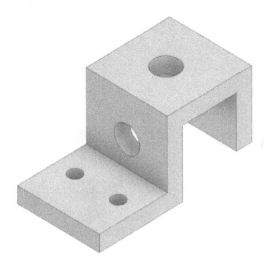

26. Click **3D Model > Modify > Chamfer** on the ribbon. On the **Chamfer** dialog, click the **Two Distances** icon. Set the **Distance 1** and **Distance 2** values to **10** and **20**, respectively.

27. Click on the right corner edge, as shown in figure.

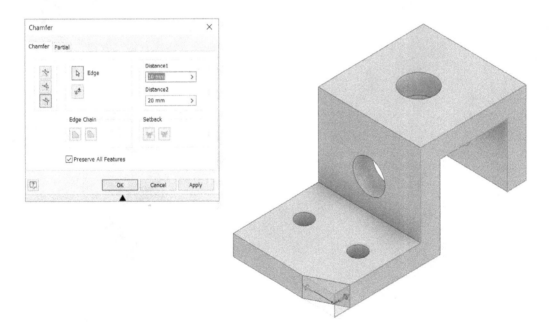

28. Click **Apply** on the dialog.
29. Click on the left edge. Click **OK** to apply the chamfer.

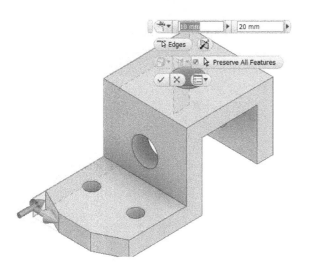

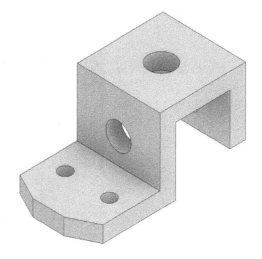

30. Click **3D Model > Modify > Fillet** on the ribbon. On the **Fillet** dialog, click the **Edge Fillet** icon. Set the **Radius** value to 8 mm and select the **Tangent Fillet** option from the **Type** drop-down.
31. Select the **Edge** option from the **Select mode** section.
32. Click on the horizontal edges of the part model, as shown below. Click **Apply** on the dialog

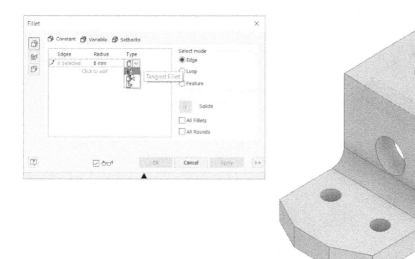

33. Type-in 20 mm in the **Radius** box.
34. Click on the outer edges of the part model, as shown below. Click **OK** to complete the fillet feature.

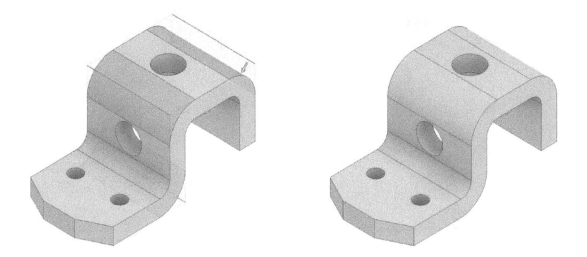

35. Click on the **Home** icon located at the top left corner of the ViewCube.

36. On the ribbon, click **3D Model > Modify > Chamfer**. On the **Chamfer** dialog, click the **Distance** icon on the left.

37. Click on the lower corner of the part model and type-in 10 in the **Distance** box. Click **Apply** to chamfer the edge.

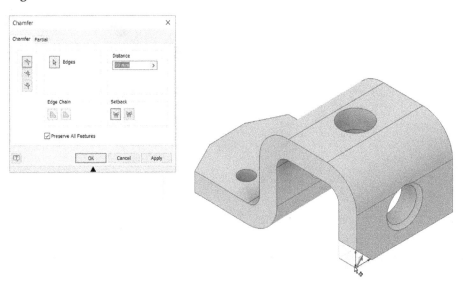

38. Likewise, select the other edge and enter 10 mm in the **Distance** box.
39. Click **OK** to chamfer the selected edge.

40. Save and close the file.

Questions

1. What are placed features?

2. How to create a counterbored hole?

3. Which option allows you to create chamfer with unequal setbacks?

4. Which option allows you to create a variable radius blend?

5. How is the size of the external thread defined?

6. How to create a Smooth Fillet?

7. How to add a unique thickness to a shell feature?

8. What is the difference between the Tapped and Taper Tapped Holes?

9. What is the use of the **Preset** drop-down of the Properties panel?

Exercises
Exercise 1 (Millimetres)

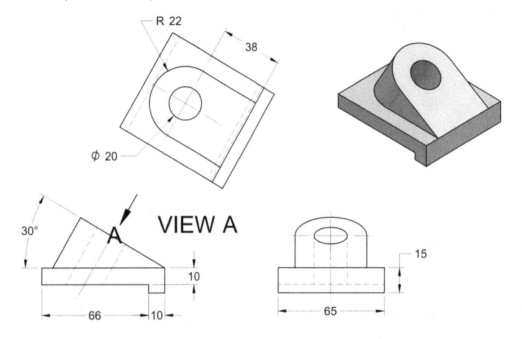

Exercise 2 (Inches)

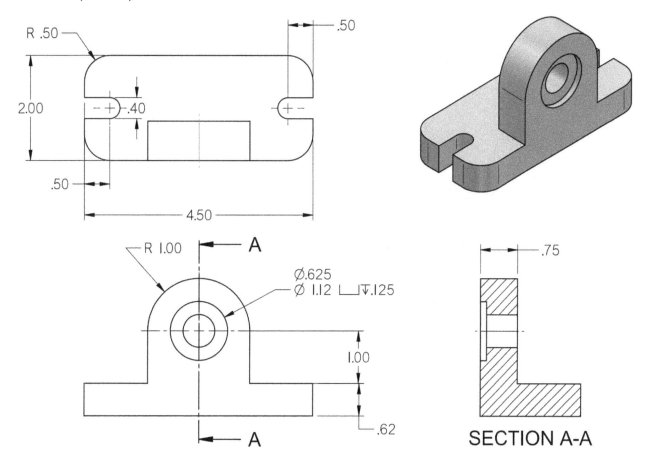

R .50

.50

2.00

.40

.50

4.50

R 1.00

A

Ø.625
Ø 1.12 ⊔↧.125

1.00

.62

A

.75

SECTION A-A

Chapter 5: Patterned Geometry

When designing a part geometry, most of the times there are elements of symmetry in each part or there are at least a few features that are repeated multiple times. In these situations, Inventor offers some commands that save your time. For example, you can use mirror features to design symmetric parts, which makes designing the part quicker. This is because you only have to design a portion of the part and use the mirror feature to create the remaining geometry.

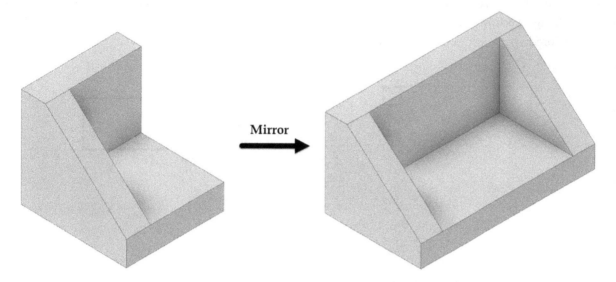

In addition, there are some pattern commands to replicate a feature throughout a part quickly. They save you time from creating additional features individually and help you modify the design easily. If the design changes, you only need to change the first feature; the rest of the pattern features will update, automatically. In this chapter, you will learn to create mirrored and pattern geometries using the commands available in Inventor.

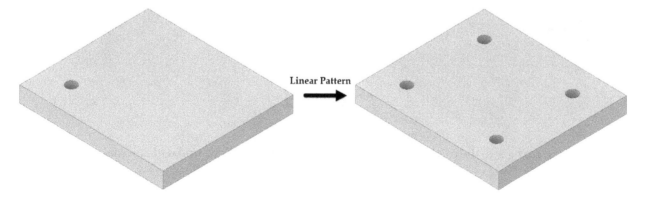

The topics covered in this chapter are:

- *Mirror* features
- *Rectangular Patterns*
- *Circular Patterns*
- *Sketch Driven Patterns*

Mirror

If you are designing a part that is symmetric, you can save time by using the **Mirror** command. Using this command, you can replicate individual features of the entire body. To mirror features (3D geometry), you need to have a face or plane to use as a reference. You can use a model face, default plane, or create a new plane, if it does not exist where it is needed.

Activate the **Mirror** command (click **3D Model > Pattern > Mirror** on the ribbon). On the **Mirror** dialog, click the **Mirror Individual Features** icon on the left. On the part geometry, click on the features to mirror, and then click the **Mirror Plane** selection button on the **Mirror** dialog. Now, select the reference plane about which the features are to be mirrored.

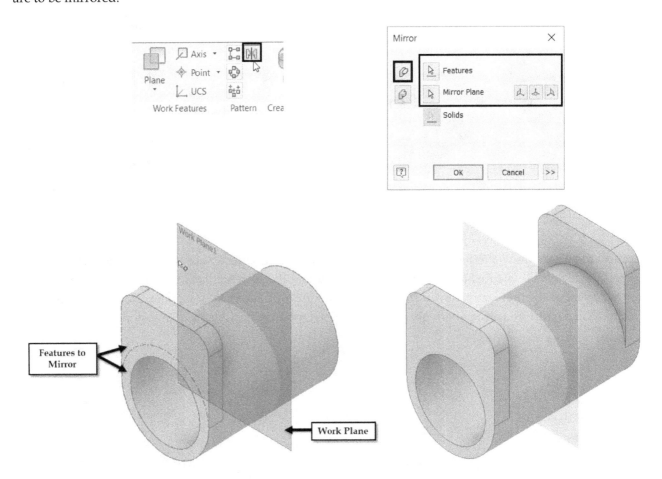

Now, if you make changes to the original feature, the mirrored feature will be updated automatically.

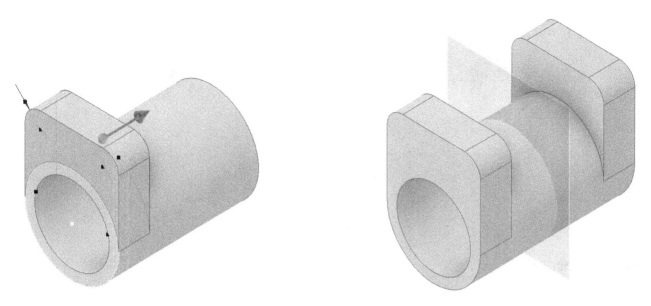

Mirror Solids

If the part you are creating is completely symmetric, you can save more time by creating half of it and mirroring the entire geometry rather than individual features. Activate the **Mirror** command (On the ribbon, click **3D Model > Pattern > Mirror**) and click **Mirror Solids** icon on the **Mirror** dialog; the solid part is selected automatically. On the **Mirror** dialog, click the **Mirror Plane** selection button and select the face about which the geometry is to be mirrored. To include other features like planes, axes, work points, surfaces and so on in the mirror feature, click the **Include Work/Surface Features** selection button and select the features. Inventor allows you to specify whether the mirrored body will be joined with the source body or to create a separate body. Click **OK** to complete the mirror geometry.

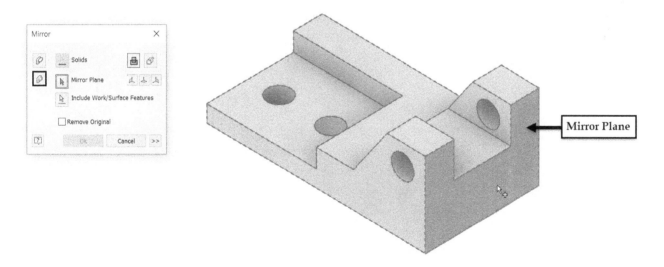

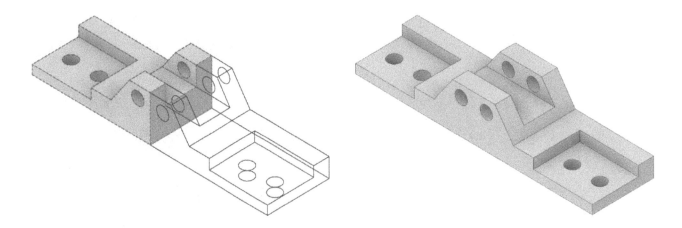

Create Patterns

Inventor allows you to replicate a feature using the pattern commands: **Rectangular Pattern**, **Circular Pattern**, and **Sketch Driven**. The following sections explain the different patterns that can be created using the three pattern commands.

Rectangular Pattern

To create a pattern in a rectangular fashion, you must first activate the **Rectangular Pattern** command (On the ribbon, click **3D Model > Pattern > Rectangular Pattern**). On the **Rectangular Pattern** dialog, click the **Pattern Individual Features** icon on the left side, and then select the feature to pattern from the model geometry. Click the **Direction 1** selection button and select **Spacing** from the drop-down. Next, select an edge, face, or axis to define the **Direction 1** of the pattern. You will notice that a pattern preview appears on the model. Type-in a value in the **Column Count** and **Column Spacing** box. Click the **Flip** icon, if you want to reverse the pattern direction. Click the **Midplane** icon to create the pattern on both sides of the source feature.

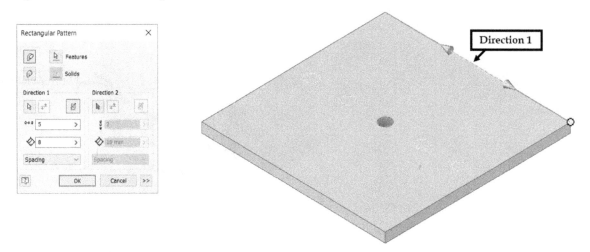

Click the **Direction 2** selection button and select an edge, face or axis to define the second direction of the pattern. Set the parameters (**Row Count** and **Row Spacing**) of the pattern in direction 2. Next, click **OK** to complete the pattern.

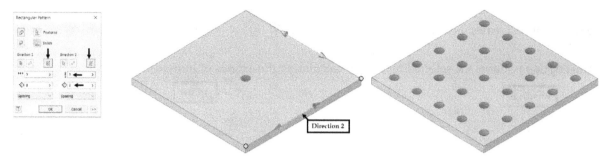

Select **Distance** from the drop-down available on the **Rectangular Pattern** dialog, if you want to enter the occurrence count and total length values along the direction 1 or direction 2.

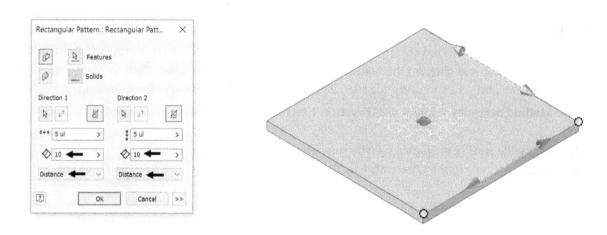

Select **Curve Length** from the drop-down available on the **Rectangular Pattern** dialog, if you want to create the pattern along the length of the curve selected to define the direction.

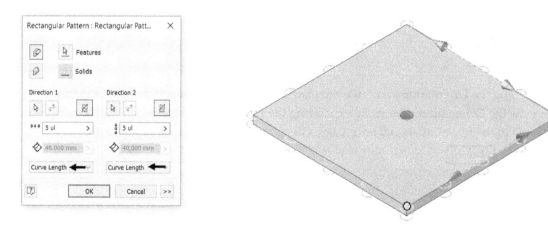

Using the Compute options

The **Compute** section has three options: **Optimized**, **Identical** and **Adjust**. You can view the **Compute** options by expanding the **Rectangular Pattern** dialog.

The **Optimized** option patterns the faces of the selected feature.

The **Identical** option creates the exact copies of the feature.

The **Adjust** option patterns the selected feature by calculating the extents of individual instances.

Creating a Pattern Along a Path

You can create a pattern along a selected curve or edge using the **Rectangular Pattern** command. Activate the **Rectangular Pattern** command and click on the feature to pattern. On the **Rectangular Pattern** dialog, click the **Direction 1** selection button and select a curve, edge or sketched path. Next, specify the **Column Count**. Select an option from the **Method** drop-down under the **Direction 1** section, and then specify the **Length** value.

Next, you need to specify the start of the pattern. To do this, first click the **More** button to expand the dialog. Click the **Start** selection button available in the **Direction 1** section and select a point or vertex to define the start point.

Select an option from the **Compute** section. The options in this section are discussed earlier.

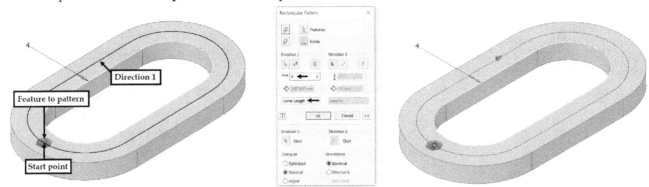

Specify the orientation using the **Orientation** section, which has three options: **Identical**, **Direction1**, and **Direction2**. You can view the **Orientation** options by expanding the **Rectangular Pattern** dialog. The options in this section are explained in the figure, as shown next. Click **OK** to create the pattern along the path.

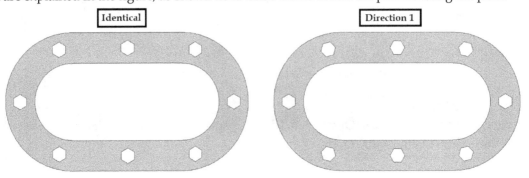

Patterning the entire geometry

The **Pattern Solids** option allows you to pattern the entire part geometry. Activate the **Rectangular Pattern** command and click the **Patter Solids** icon on the dialog. Next, define the direction, occurrence count, and spacing between the instances. There is no need to select the geometry as the entire body is selected by default.

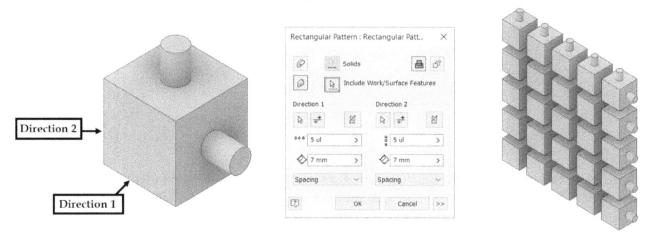

Suppressing Occurrences

If you want to suppress an occurrence of the pattern, then expand the **Rectangular Pattern** feature in the Model window. Next, place the pointer on an occurrence; it is highlighted in the graphics window. Likewise, identify the occurrence to be suppressed. Next, right-click on it and select **Suppress**.

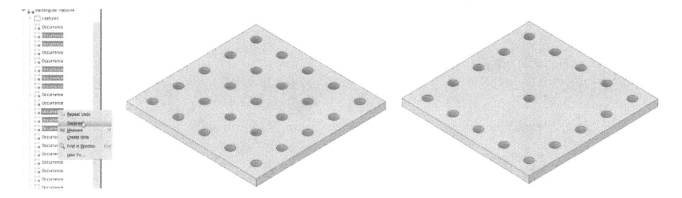

Circular Pattern

The circular pattern is used to pattern the selected features in a circular fashion. Activate the circular pattern command (click **3D Model > Pattern > Circular Pattern** on the ribbon) and select the feature to pattern from the model geometry. Click on the **Rotation Axis** selection button and select the axis from the model geometry or click on a cylindrical face; the axis of the rotation is defined. Usually, the axis of rotation is perpendicular to the plane/face on which the selected feature is placed.

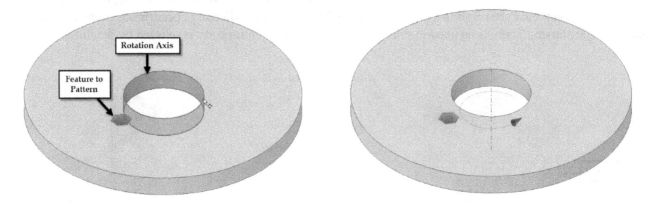

Click the **More** button to expand the **Circular Pattern** dialog. Under the **Positioning Method** section, select the **Fitted** option. Type-in values in the **Occurrence Count** and **Occurrence Angle** boxes of the **Placement** section. The total number of occurrences you specify will be fitted in the occurrence angle.

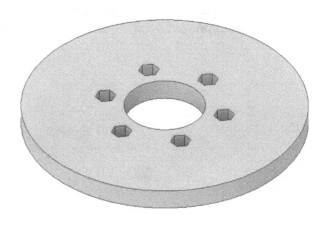

Select **Positioning Method > Incremental**, if you want to type-in the occurrence count and the angle between individual instances.

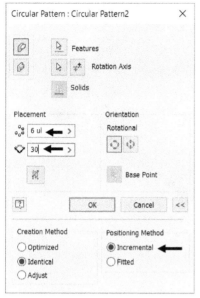

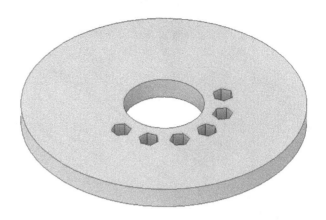

Under the **Orientation** section, click **Rotational** icon to change the orientation of the instances, as they are patterned in the circular fashion. Click **Fixed** icon, if you want to pattern the feature with the original orientation.

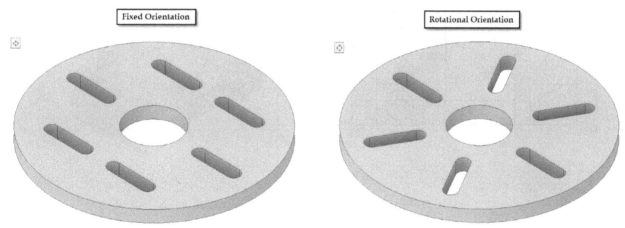

Sketch Driven Pattern

The **Sketch Driven** command is used to pattern the feature or body by using the sketch points. Activate this command (click **3D Model > Pattern > Sketch Driven Pattern** on the ribbon). Next, select the feature to pattern; the sketch is selected automatically and the preview of the pattern is displayed. Under the **Reference** section, click the **Base Point** selection button and select a point to define the base point of the pattern. Click **OK** to create the pattern

 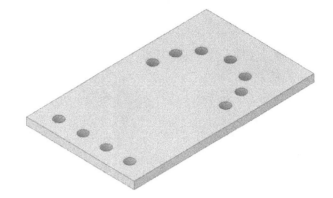

Examples

Example 1 (Millimeters)

In this example, you will create the part shown below.

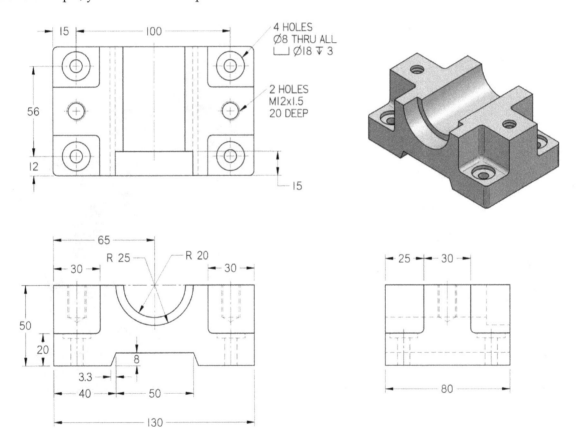

1. Start **Autodesk Inventor 2019.**
2. Open a new file using the **Standard (mm).ipt** template.
3. To start a sketch, click **3D Model > Sketch > Start 2D Sketch** on the ribbon. Click on the **XY** plane.
4. Create a rectangular sketch, add dimensions as shown and click **Finish Sketch** on the ribbon.
5. Activate the **Extrude** command.

6. On the **Extrude** dialog, select **Distance** from the **Extents** drop-down and type-in 80 in the **Distance1** box. Click **Symmetric** icon under the **Extents** section and click **OK** to complete the Extrude feature.

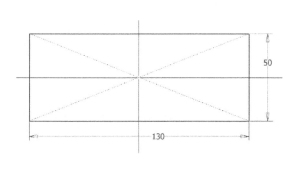 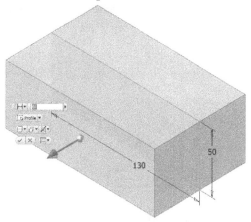

7. Click **3D Model > Sketch > Start 2D Sketch**, on the ribbon.
8. Click on the top face of the part model, as shown in figure. Next, the draw sketch as shown. Click **Sketch > Exit > Finish Sketch**, on the ribbon.

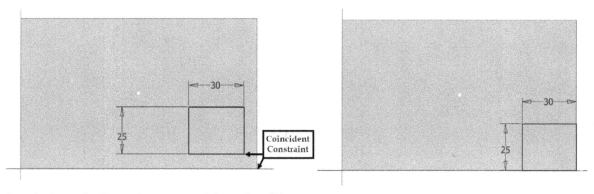

9. Activate the **Extrude** command from the ribbon.
10. On the **Extrude** dialog, click the **Cut** icon and select **Extents > Distance**. Type-in 30 in the **Distance** box and click **OK** to create the *Cutout* feature.

 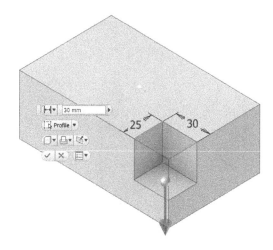

11. Activate the **Create 2D Sketch** command and click on the top face of the *Cutout* feature.

12. Click **Sketch > Create > Point** on the ribbon and place the point.

13. On the ribbon, click **Sketch > Constrain > Horizontal Constraint** 〰 . Select the point and the midpoint of the right vertical edge; the selected points are aligned horizontally.

14. On the ribbon, click **Sketch > Constrain > Vertical Constraint** ⫴ . Select the point and the midpoint of the bottom horizontal edge of the cutout; the selected points are aligned vertically.

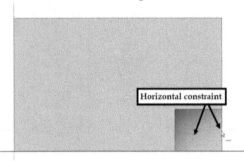
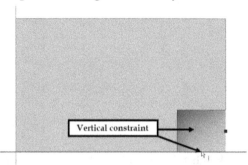

15. Click **Finish Sketch** on the ribbon.

16. Activate the **Hole** command and place the counterbore hole on the *Cutout* feature.

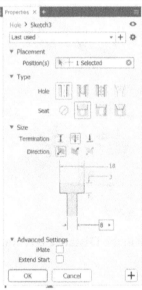
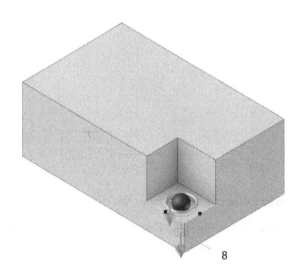

17. Click **OK** to complete the *Hole* feature.

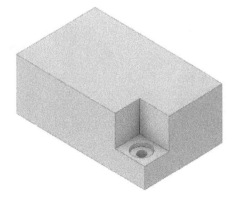

18. Click **3D Model > Pattern > Rectangular Pattern**, on the ribbon.
19. On the **Rectangular Pattern** dialog, click the **Features** selection button and select the *Hole* and *Cutout* features.
20. Click the **Direction 1** selection button and click on the top front edge of the part model.
21. Type in **2** and **100** in the **Column Count** and **Column Spacing** boxes, respectively.
22. Click the **Direction 2** selection button and click on the top side edge of the part model.
23. Type in **2** and **55** in the **Column Count** and **Column Spacing** boxes, respectively. Click **OK** to complete the pattern feature.

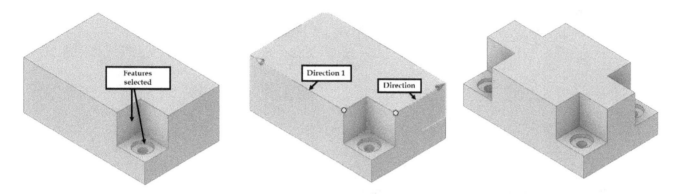

24. Click **3D Model > Sketch > Start 2D Sketch**, on the ribbon. Click on the front face of the part model.
25. Click **Sketch > Create > Point**, on the ribbon. Place a point and apply the **Coincident Constraint** between the point and the midpoint of the top edge, as shown. Click **Finish Sketch** on the ribbon.

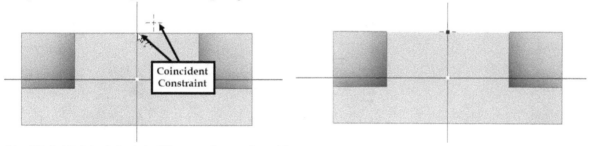

26. Click **3D Model > Modify > Hole**, on the ribbon.
27. On the **Properties panel**, click **Type > Hole > Simple Hole**.
28. Click **Type > Seat > Counterbore** on the **Properties** panel.
29. Click **Size > Termination > Through All**. Set **Direction** to **Default**.
30. Type-in **50** and **15** mm in the **Counterbore Diameter** and **Counterbore Depth** boxes, respectively.
31. Set the **Diameter** value to **40** mm and click **OK** to create the counterbore hole.

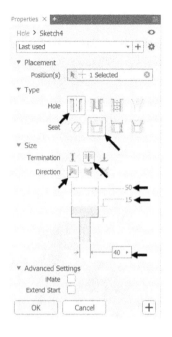

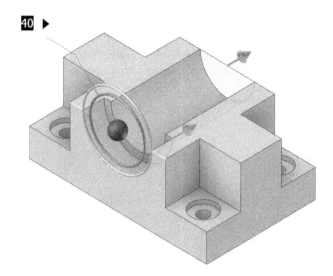

32. Click **3D Model > Modify > Hole**, on the ribbon and click on the top face of the part model, as shown.
33. On the Properties Panel, click **Type > Hole > Tapped Hole**, and set the parameters, as shown in figure.

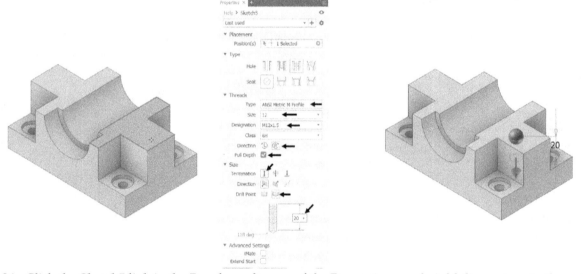

34. Click the **Sketch5** link in the Breadcrumbs area of the Properties panel. Add dimensions to the point and click **Finish Sketch**.

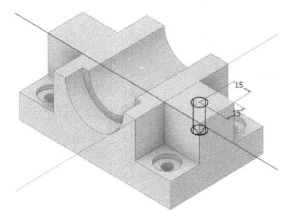
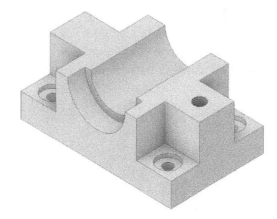

35. On the ribbon, click **3D Model > Pattern > Mirror** .
36. On the **Mirror** dialog, click the **Features** button and select the threaded hole feature from the part model.
37. Click the **Origin YZ plane** icon on the **Mirror** dialog. Click **OK** to complete the mirror feature.

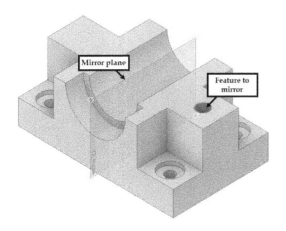
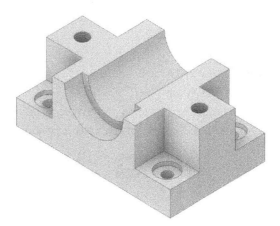

38. Activate the **Create 2D Sketch** command and click on the front face of the part model.
39. Draw the sketch and add dimensions, as shown in figure. Note that you should apply the **Symmetric** constraint between the two inclined lines. Click **Finish Sketch** on the ribbon.
40. Create a *Cutout* throughout the part model, as shown.

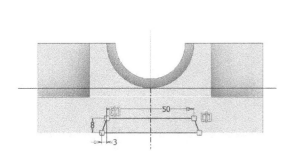
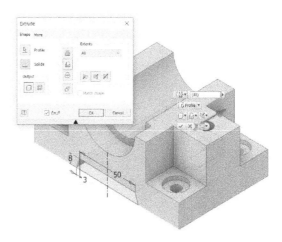

41. On the ribbon, click **3D Model > Modify > Fillet**.

42. On the **Fillet** dialog, select **Select Mode > Edge**, and then click on the edges of the cutout feature; the edges are filleted. Type 2 in the **Radius** box available on the **Fillet** dialog.

43. Likewise, select the edges of the remaining cutout features. Click **OK**.

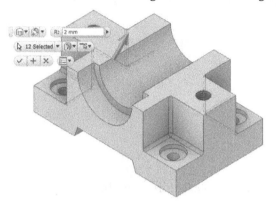 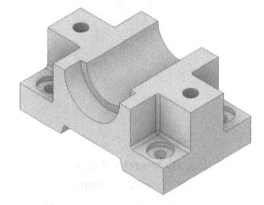

44. Save and close the part file.

Questions

1. Describe the procedure to create a mirror feature.
2. List any two pattern types.
3. Describe the procedure to create a pattern along curve.
4. List the methods to define spacing in a Rectangular pattern.

Exercises

Exercise 1 (Millimetres)

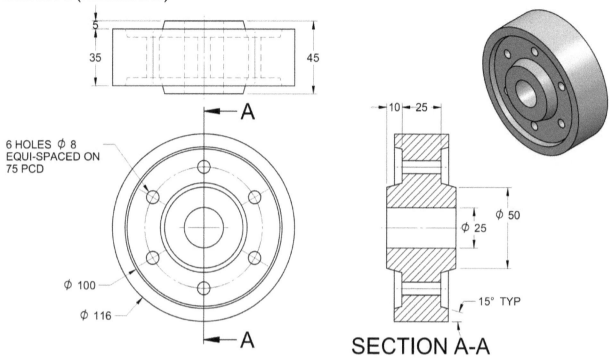

6 HOLES ∅ 8
EQUI-SPACED ON
75 PCD

∅ 100

∅ 116

A

A

10 25

∅ 50

∅ 25

15° TYP

SECTION A-A

5

35

45

Chapter 6: Sweep Features

The **Sweep** command is one of the basic commands available in Inventor that allow you to generate solid geometry. It can be used to create simple geometry as well as complex shapes. A sweep is composed of two items: a cross-section and a path. The cross-section controls the shape of sweep while the path controls its direction. For example, take a look at the angled cylinder shown in figure. This is created using a simple sweep with the circle as the profile and an angled line as the path.

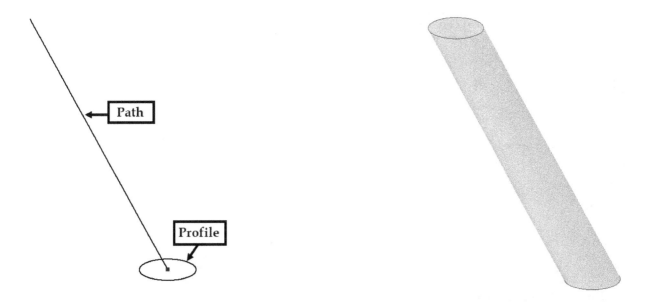

By making the path a bit more complex, you can see that a sweep allows you to create shapes you would not be able to create using commands such as Extrude or Revolve.

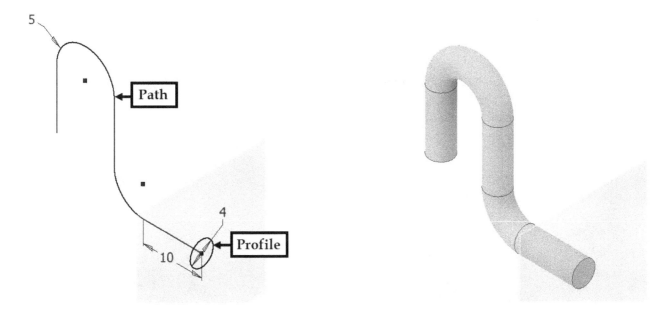

To take the sweep feature to the next level of complexity, you can add guide rails and guide surface. By doing so, the shape of the geometry is controlled by guide rails and surface. For example, the circular cross-section in figure varies in size along the path because a guide rail controls it.

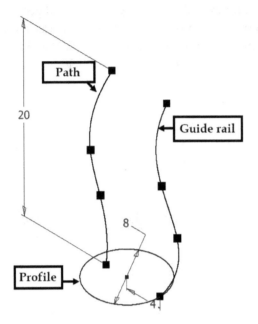 

The topics covered in this chapter are:

- *Path sweeps*
- *Path and Guide rail sweeps*
- *Path and Guide Surface sweeps*
- *Scaling and twisting the cross-section along the path*
- *Swept Cutouts*
- *Coils*

Path sweeps

This type of sweep requires two elements: a path and profile. The profile defines the shape of the sweep along the path. A path is used to control the direction of the profile. A path can be a sketch or an edge. To create a sweep, you must first create a path and a profile. Create a path by drawing a sketch. It can be an open or closed sketch. Next, click **3D Model > Work Features > Planes drop-down > Normal to Curve at Point** on the ribbon, and then create a plane normal to the path. Sketch the profile on the plane normal to the path.

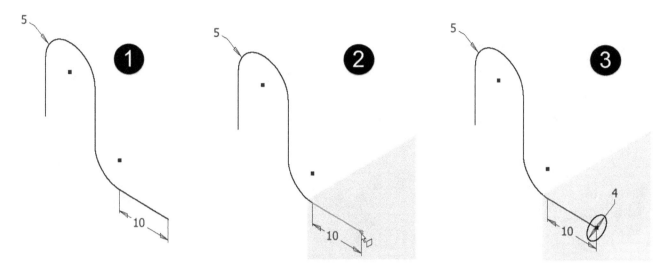

Activate the **Sweep** command (click **3D Model > Create > Sweep** on the ribbon). As you activate this command, a dialog appears showing different options to create the sweep. Select the **Path** option from the **Type** drop-down on the dialog. If there is any closed sketch in the graphics window, it will be selected as the profile, automatically. Next, select the path and click **OK**.

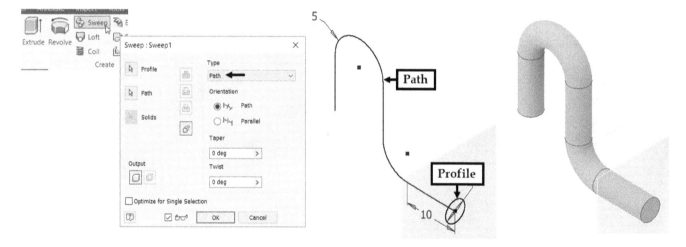

Inventor will not allow the sweep to result in a self-intersecting geometry. As the profile is swept along a path, it cannot comeback and cross itself. For example, if the profile of the sweep is larger than the curves on the path, the resulting geometry will intersect and the sweep will fail.

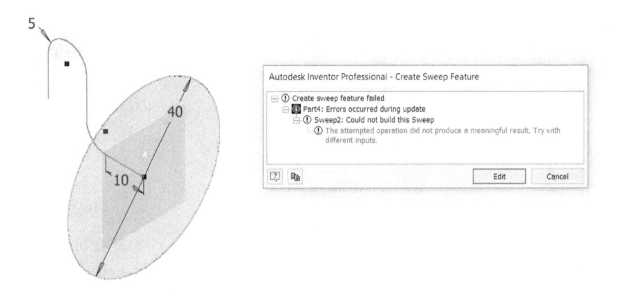

A sweep profile must be created as a sketch. However, a path can be a sketch or an edge. The following illustrations show various types of paths and resultant sweep features.

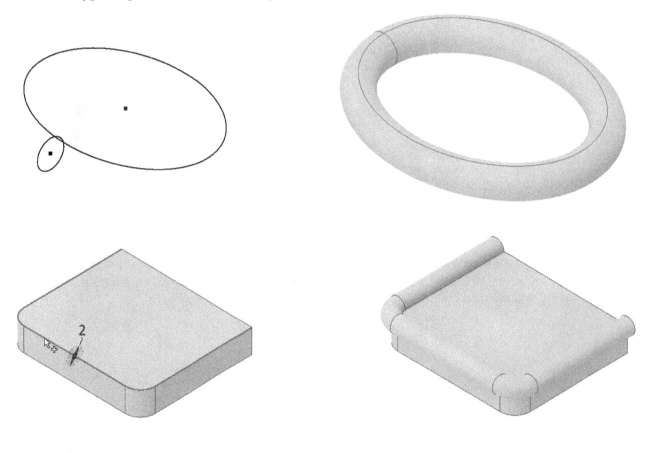

Profile Orientation

The **Orientation** options define the orientation of the resulting geometry. The **Path** option sweeps the cross-section in the direction normal to the path. The **Parallel** option sweeps the cross-section in the direction parallel to itself.

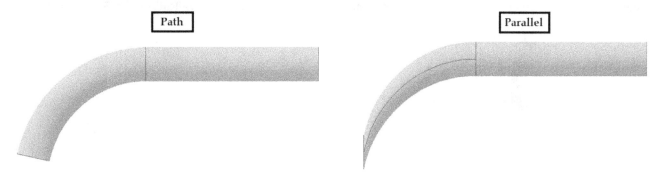

Taper

Inventor allows you to taper the sweep along the path. Select the profile and path, and then type-in a value in the **Taper** box. Click **OK** to create the tapered sweep feature.

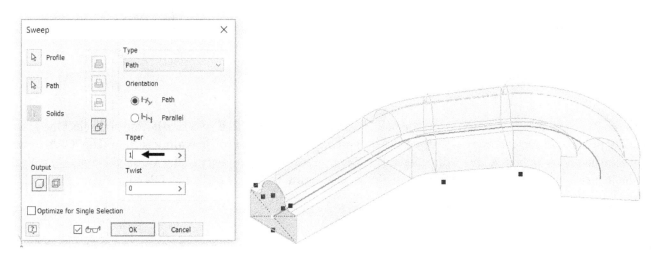

Twist

Inventor allows you to twist the profile along the path. Define the path and profile, and then type-in the twist angle in the **Twist** box; the twist is applied to the profile.

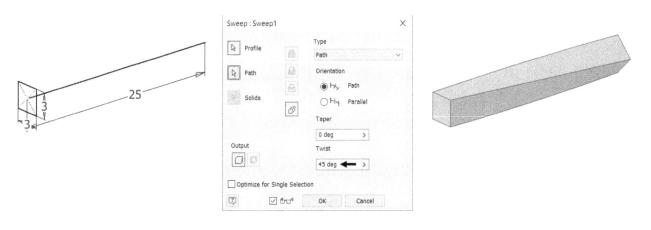

Path and Guide Rail Sweeps

Inventor allows you to create sweep features with path and guide rails. This can be useful while creating complex geometry and shapes. To create this type of sweep feature, first create a path. Next, create a profile and guide rail, as shown in figure. Activate the **Sweep** command and select **Type > Path & Guide Rail** on the **Sweep** dialog; the profile is selected, automatically.

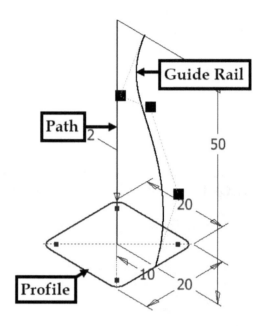

Click the **Path** selection button and select the path. Next, click the **Guide Rail** selection button and select the guide rail. The preview of the geometry will appear. Select an option from the **Profile scaling** section. The **X &Y** option scales the geometry in both X and Y directions. The **X** option scales the geometry in the **X** direction only. The **None** option just sweeps the profile along the path without considering the guide rail. Click **OK** to complete the feature.

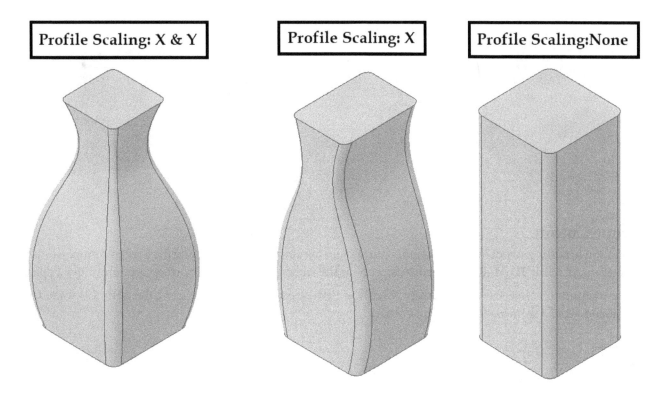

Path and Guide Surface Sweeps

The **Path & Guide Surface** option on the **Sweep** dialog will be useful while sweeping a profile along a non-planar path. For example, create a path and profile similar to the one shown in figure. Next, create a sweep feature using the **Path** option; the sweep is not attached to the cylindrical surface.

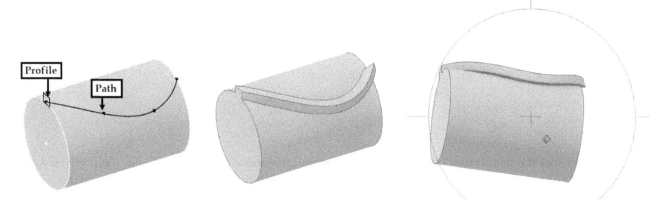

Now, right click on the **Sweep** feature in the **Model** window and select **Edit Feature**. On the **Sweep** dialog, select **Type > Path & Guide Surface**, and then select the cylindrical surface to define the guide surface. Click **OK** and notice that the sweep feature is attached to the surface.

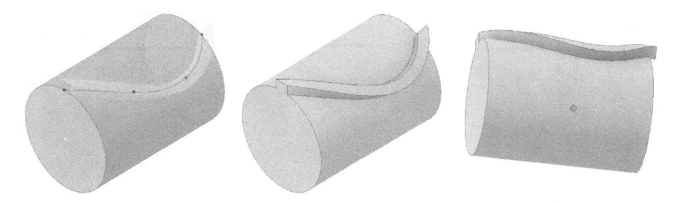

Swept Cutout

In addition to adding swept features, Inventor allows you to remove geometry using the **Sweep** command. Activate this command (click **3D Model > Create > Sweep** on the ribbon) and select the sweep type from the **Type** drop-down; the profile is selected automatically. Click the **Path** selection button and select the path. Click the **Cut** ⬚ icon dialog. Click **OK** to create the swept cutout.

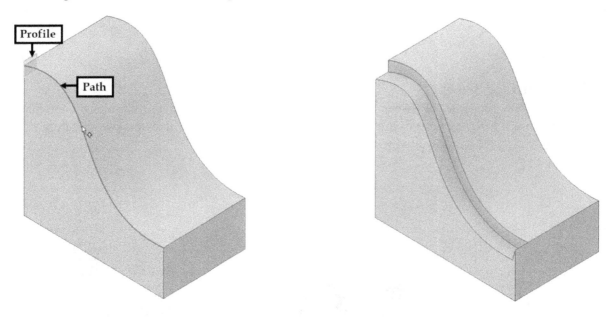

You will notice that the swept cutout is not created throughout the geometry. This is because the profile is swept only up to the endpoints of the path. In this case, you must edit the path such that it extends beyond the geometry. Expand the **Sweep** feature in the Model window and notice that a 3D sketch is created from the selected model edge. Right click on the 3D sketch and select **Edit 3D Sketch**. Next, create a line that is continuous and collinear with the path. Click **Finish Sketch** on the ribbon. Now, right click on the **Sweep** feature in the **Model** window and select **Edit Feature**. Click the **Path** selection button on the **Sweep** dialog, and then select the newly created line. Click **OK** to complete the feature. The resultant swept cutout will be throughout the geometry.

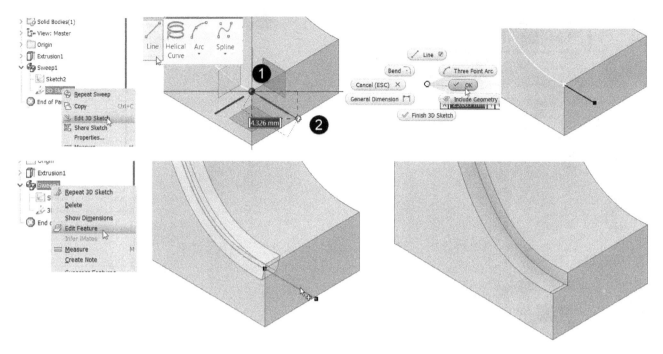

Coil

This command creates a spring or spiral shaped feature. To create this type of feature, you must have a profile and a line (axis). They can be on a same plane or on different planes. Activate the **Coil** command (click **3D Model > Create > Coil** on the ribbon); the profile is selected, automatically. Click the **Axis** selection button and select a line or axis; the preview of the coil appears on the screen.

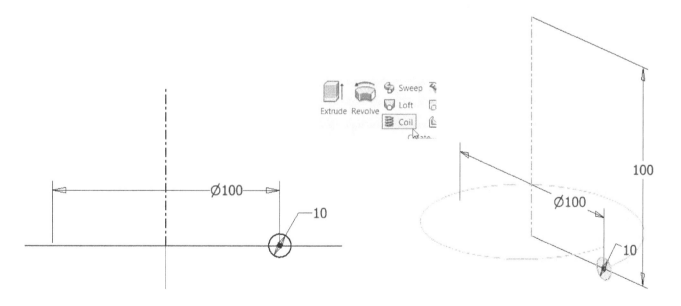

Click anyone of the icons available in the **Rotation** section; this defines the coil direction.

Left Hand Coil

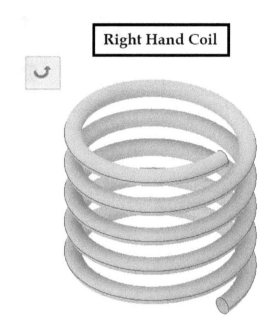

Right Hand Coil

Now, click the **Coil Size** tab on the **Coil** dialog and select an option from the **Type** drop-down. There are four options in this drop-down: **Pitch and Revolution**, **Revolution and Height**, **Pitch and Height**, and **Spiral**.

The **Pitch and Height** option creates a helical coil by using the total height of the coil and the distance between the turns. You need to specify the **Height** and **Pitch** values.

The **Revolution and Height** option creates a helical coil by using the total height of the coil and number of turns.

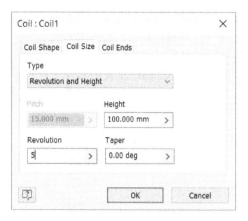

The **Pitch and Revolution** option uses the pitch and number of revolutions you specify to create the coil.

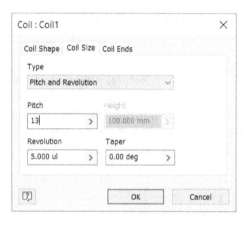

The **Spiral** option creates a spiral shaped feature.

The **Taper** box on the **Coil Size** tab helps you to apply taper to the coil. You can apply taper to a coil by entering the angle. The positive or negative angle values define the taper direction.

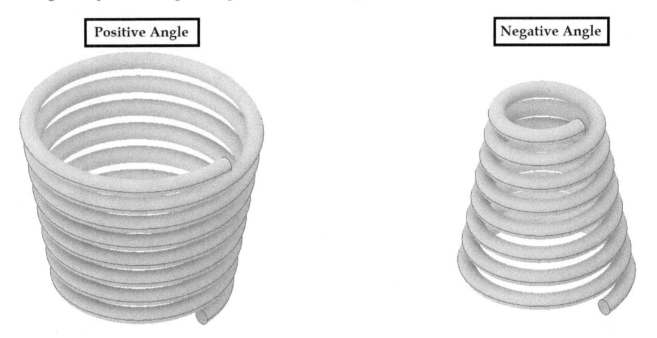

Click the **Coil Ends** tab and specify the transition type for start and end of the coil. The **Natural** option creates a coil without any transition. The **Flat** option creates a flat transition so that the coil can stand upright on a flat surface. The **Transition Angle** box is used to specify the transition distance beyond the coil. The transition distance will be less than one revolution. The **Flat Angle** box is used to specify the distance of the flat portion that extends beyond the transition.

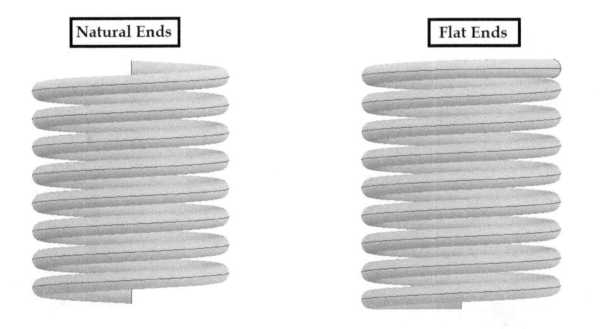

Click **OK** on the **Coil** dialog to create the coil.

Helical Cutout

The **Coil** command can also be used to remove material from the part geometry by creating a helical feature. To create this feature, first you must have an existing geometry, and the sketches of the profile and axis. Activate this command (click **3D Model > Create > Coil** on the ribbon) and select the profile. Click the **Axis** selection button and select the axis. Click the **Cut** icon on the **Coil** dialog. Define the number of turns and pitch, and then click **OK** to create the helical cutout.

Examples

Example 1 (Inches)

In this example, you will create the part shown below.

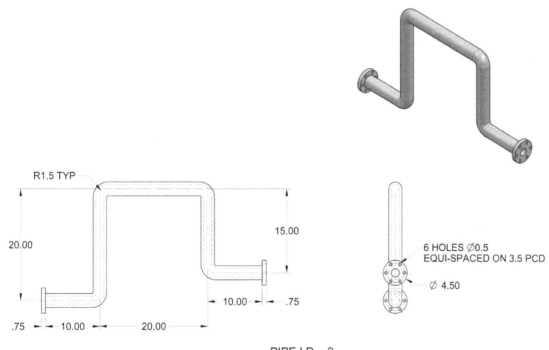

PIPE I.D. - 2
PIPE O.D. - 2.5

175

1. Start **Autodesk Inventor**.
2. On the **Quick Access Toolbar**, click **New**; the **Create New File** dialog pops up.
3. On this dialog, click **Templates > en-US**. Select the **Standard.ipt** template and click **Create**.
4. On the ribbon, click **3D Model > Sketch > Create 2D Sketch** and draw the sketch on the XY plane, as shown below.

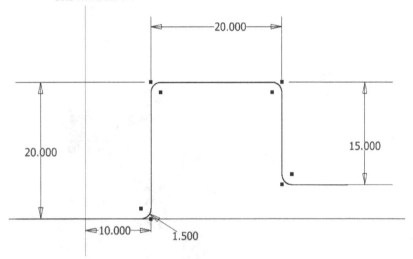

5. Click **Finish Sketch** on the ribbon.

6. On the ribbon, click **3D Model > Work Features > Planes** drop-down > **Normal to Curve at Point** and click on the lower horizontal line.
7. Click on the endpoint of the line to locate the plane.

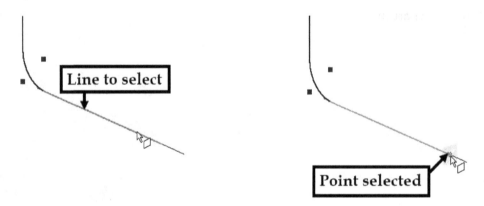

8. On the ribbon, click **3D Model > Sketch > Create 2D Sketch**, and then select the plane normal to the curve.
9. On the ribbon, click **Sketch > Create > Circle Center Point** and draw a circle of 2.5 inch diameter. Click **Finish Sketch**.

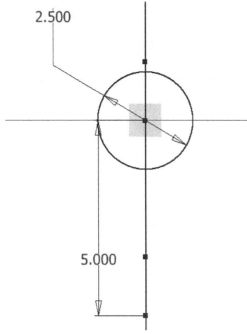

10. On the ribbon, click **3D Model > Create > Sweep**; the **Sweep** dialog pops up. On this dialog, select **Type > Path**.

11. Click the **Path** selection button, and then click on the first sketch to define the path of the *Sweep* feature. Click **OK** to complete the *Sweep* feature.

12. On the ribbon, click **3D Model > Modify > Shell**. Click on the end face of the *Sweep* feature.
13. Rotate the part geometry and click on the end face on the other side.
14. Type-in **0.5** in the **Thickness** box. Click **OK** to shell the *Sweep* feature.

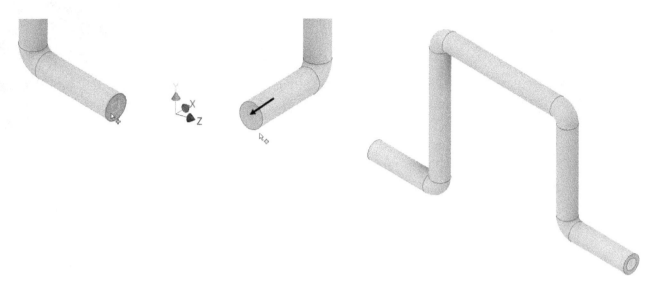

15. On the ribbon, click **3D Model > Sketch > Create 2D Sketch** and click on the front end face.
16. On the ribbon, click **Sketch > Create > Project Geometry**. Click on the inner edge of the end face to project it.
17. Draw a circle of 4.5 in diameter. Click **Finish Sketch** on the ribbon.

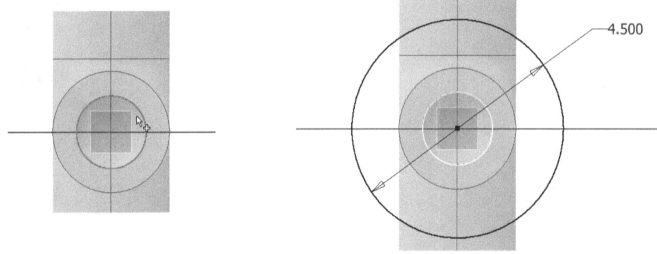

18. Activate the **Extrude** command and click inside the sketch region, as shown. Type-in 0.75 in the **Distance1** box. Press Enter to create the flange.

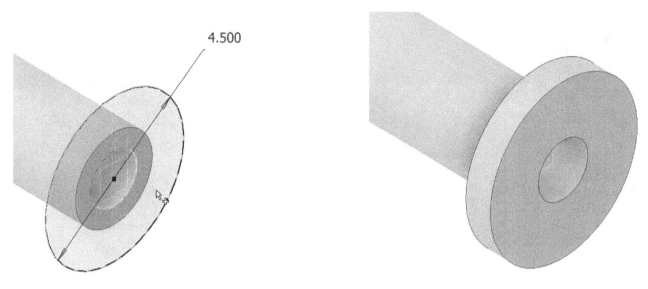

19. Create a simple hole of 0.5 diameter on the extruded face.

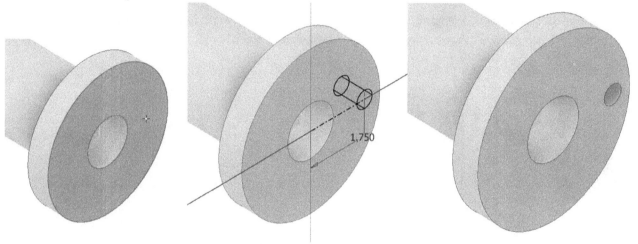

20. On the ribbon, click **3D Model > Pattern > Circular Pattern** . Click the **Pattern Individual Features** icon and select the hole feature from the geometry. Now, you have to define the axis of the circular pattern.
21. Click the **Rotation Axis** selection button and select cylindrical face of the extruded feature. This defines the pattern axis.
22. Type-in **6** in the **Occurrence Count** box and click **OK** on the dialog. The hole is patterned in a circular fashion.

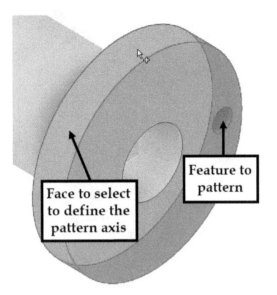

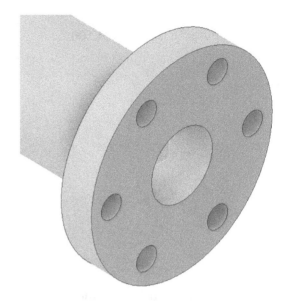

23. Change the model view orientation, as shown. Start a sketch on the end face of the *Sweep* feature, and then create a sketch point, as shown. Next, click **Finish Sketch** on the ribbon.

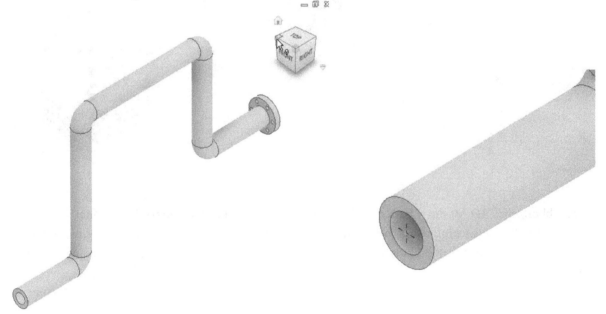

24. On the ribbon, click **3D Model > Pattern > Sketch Driven** ; the sketch point is selected, automatically.
25. Select the extruded feature and the circular pattern.
26. Click the **Base Point** selection button on the **Sketch Driven Pattern** dialog. Select the circular edge of the extruded feature, a shown. Its center point is selected as the base point.
27. Click **OK** to create sketch driven pattern.

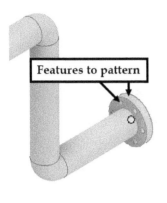

Features to pattern

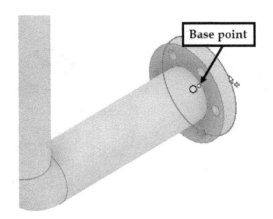

Base point

28. Save and close the part file.

Questions

1. List the methods to create the *Sweep* features.

2. How to apply twist and turns to *Sweep* features?

3. How is the **Path and Guide Surface** option useful?

4. List any two options to define the size of the coil features.

Exercises
Exercise 1

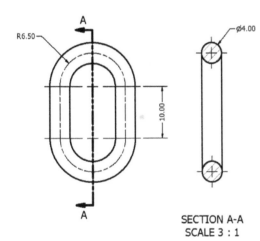

R6.50

A

10.00

A

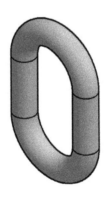

Ø4.00

SECTION A-A
SCALE 3 : 1

Exercise 2

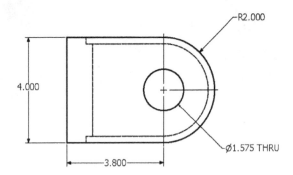

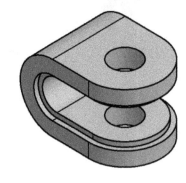

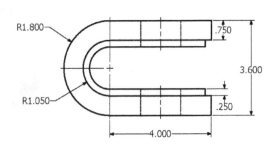

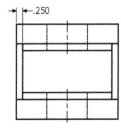

Chapter 7: Loft Features

The **Loft** command is one of the advanced commands available in Inventor that allows you to create simple as well as complex shapes. A basic loft is created by defining two cross-sections and joining them together. For example, if you create a loft feature between a circle and a square, you can easily change the cross-sectional shape of the solid. This ability is what separates the loft feature from the sweep feature.

The topics covered in this chapter are:

- *Basic Lofts*
- *Loft sections*
- *Conditions*
- *Rails*
- *Closed Loop*
- *Center Line Loft*
- *Area Loft*
- *Loft Cutouts*

Loft

This command creates a loft feature between different cross-sections. To create a loft, first create two or more sections on different planes. The planes can be parallel or perpendicular to each other. Activate the **Loft** command (click **3D Model > Create > Loft** on the ribbon); the **Loft** dialog appears. Now, you need to select two or more cross-sections that will define the loft. On the dialog, click in the **Sections** area, and then select the cross-sections from the graphics window. Click **OK** to create the loft.

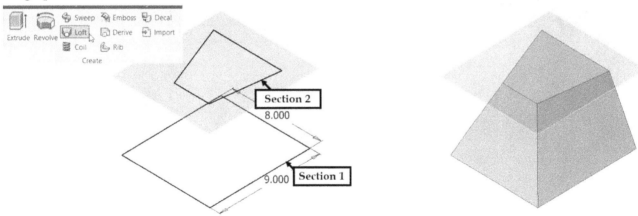

Loft sections

In addition to 2D sketches, you can also define loft cross-sections by using different element types. For instance, you can use existing model faces, surfaces, and points. The only restriction is that the points can be used at the beginning or end of a loft.

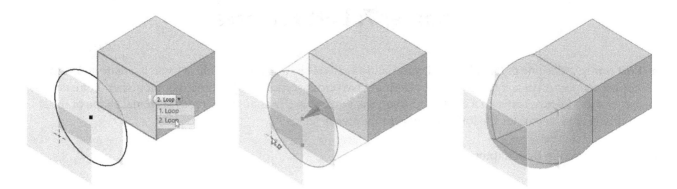

Conditions

The shape of a simple loft is controlled by the cross-sections and the plane location. However, the **Conditions** tab options can control the behaviour of the side faces. If you would like to change the shape of the side faces, you can use the **Conditions** tab options either at the beginning of the loft, the end of the lofts or both.

Direction Condition

Click the **Conditions** tab and select **Direction Condition** from the drop-down located next to the first section. Next, enter 60 in the **Angle** box; the preview of the loft updates. You can notice that the beginning of the loft starts at an angle of 60 degrees to the cross-section. You can control how much influence the angle will have by adjusting the parameter in the **Weight** box. A lower value will have lesser effect on the feature. As you increase the value, the more noticeable the effect will be, eventually. If you increase the number high enough, the direction angle will lead to self-intersecting results.

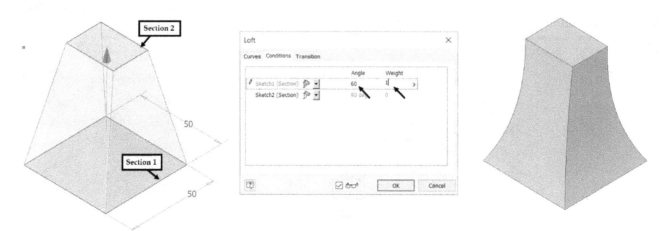

Loft Features

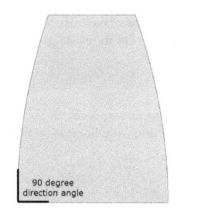 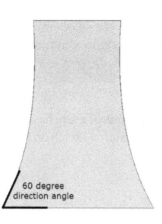 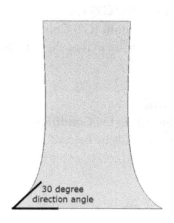

Likewise, you can also apply the direction condition to the second cross-section of the loft.

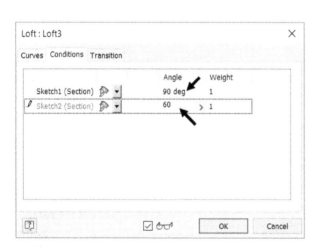 

Tangent Condition

The **Tangent Condition** 🖐 option is available when you select an existing face loop as one of the cross section. This option makes the side faces of the loft feature tangent to the side faces of the existing geometry.

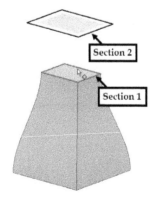  

Smooth (G2) Condition

The **Smooth (G2) Condition** option is available when you select an existing face loop as one of the cross section. This option makes the side faces of the loft feature curvature continuous with the side faces of the existing geometry.

Rails

Similar to the **Condition** options, rails allow you to control the behaviour of a loft between cross-sections. You can create rails by using 2D or 3D sketches. For example, start a sketch on the plane intersecting with the cross-sections, and then create a spline, as shown.

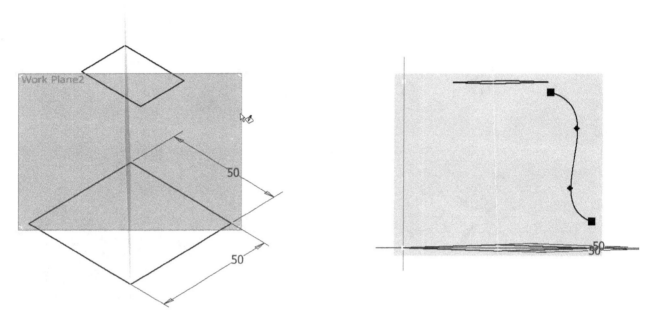

Next, you need to connect the end points of the spline with the cross-sections. To do this, click **Sketch > Create > Project Geometry** on the ribbon, and project the end points of the cross-sections onto the sketch plane. Next, apply the **Coincident Constraint** between the end points of the spline and the projected elements. Click **Finish Sketch** on the ribbon.

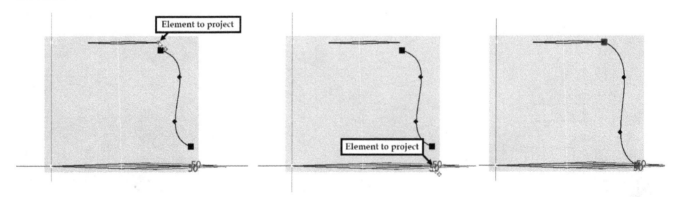

Likewise, create a sketch on the other plane, as shown. Next, click **Finish Sketch**.

Loft Features

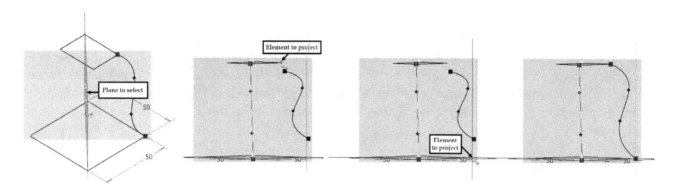

Now, activate the **Loft** command and select the cross-sections. To select rails, click in the **Rails** section and select the first rail. Next, click the **Click to add** option in the **Rails** section and select the other rails; you will see that the preview updates. Notice that the edges with rails are affected.

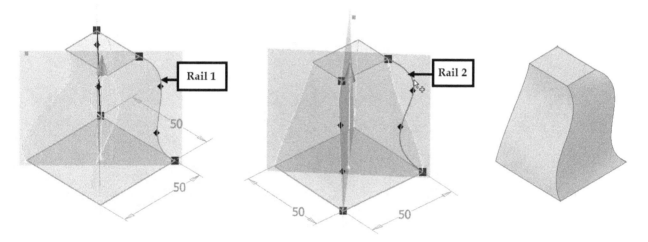

Closed Loop

Inventor allows you to create a loft that closes on itself. For example, to create a model that lofts between each of the shapes, you must select four sketches as shown in figure, and then check the **Closed Loop** option on the dialog. Next, click **OK**; this will give you a closed loft.

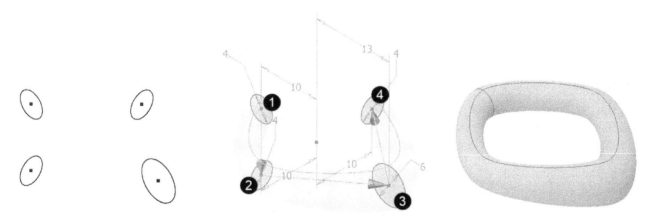

Center Line Loft

In the previous section, you have created a closed loft using four sections. However, the transition between the sections was not smooth. The **Center Line** option helps you to create a smooth transition between the sections. First, create a centerline passing through all the sections, as shown. Next, activate the **Loft** command and select the **Center Line** option, and then select the center line. Click in the **Section** area and select the loft sections; the preview of the loft appears. Check the **Closed Loop** option, if you want to create a closed loop, and then click **OK**.

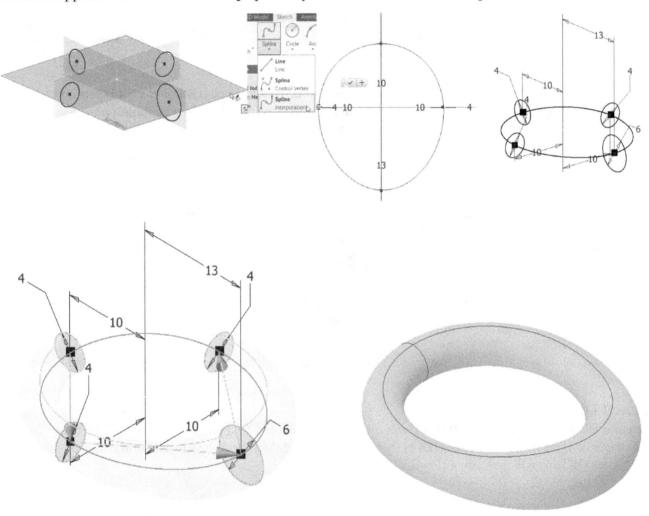

Area Loft

The **Area Loft** option allows you to create a loft without creating multiple planes and cross-sections. You need to have start and end cross sections, and a centerline. Activate the **Loft** command and select the **Area Loft** option from the **Loft** dialog. Select the start and end cross-sections, and then click in the **Center Line** area and select the centerline; the preview of the loft feature appears.

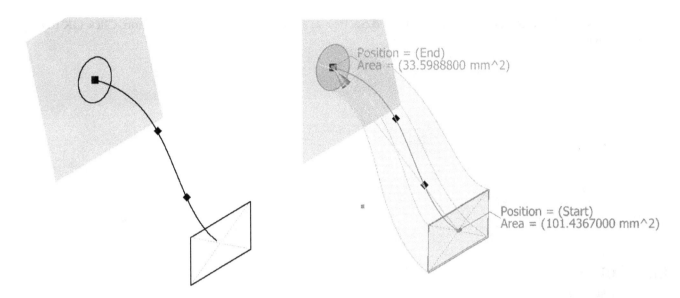

Click in the **Placed Sections** area and click on the center line to place a section; the **Section Dimensions** dialog appears. On this dialog, specify the section position using the **Section Position** options: **Proportional Distance** and **Absolute Distance**. The **Proportional Distance** option allows you to specify the location by entering a value between 0 and 1. The zero value specifies the location at the start point of the center line. Whereas the 1 value places the section at the endpoint. The **Absolute Distance** option allows you to enter the exact distance at which the section will be positioned. In this case, select the **Proportional Distance** option and enter **0.5** in the box.

The **Driving Section** option allows you to place a section and specify its size. The **Driven Section** option allows you to only place the section. The size of the placed section will be driven by the start and end sections. In this case, select the **Driving Section** option.

Next, select an option from the **Section Size** section. The **Area** option allows you to enter the area the placed section. Whereas, the **Scale Factor** option allows you to enter the scale factor. The area of the placed section is scale by the value that you enter. For example, if you enter 0.9 in the **Scale Factor** box, the area of the placed section will be scaled by 0.9 times. This in case, select the **Scale Factor** option and enter 0.9 as the scale factor. Click **OK** to apply the position and size values of the placed section. You can change the values of the placed section by double-clicking on the values displayed on it.

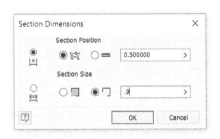

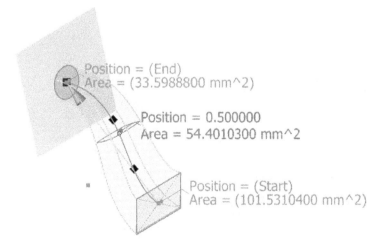

189

Likewise, click the **Click to add** option in the **Placed Section** area, and then add another section. Click **OK** to complete the feature.

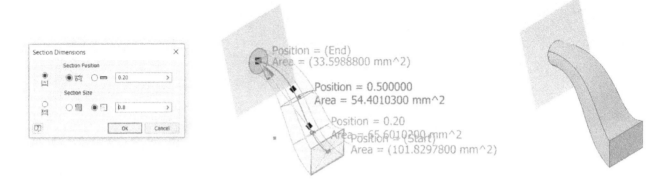

Loft Cutout

Like other standard features such as extrude, revolve and sweep, the loft feature can be used to add or remove material. You can remove material by using the **Loft** command. Activate this command (click **3D Model > Create > Loft** on the ribbon) and select the cross-sections. Click **Cut** and **OK** to create the loft cutout.

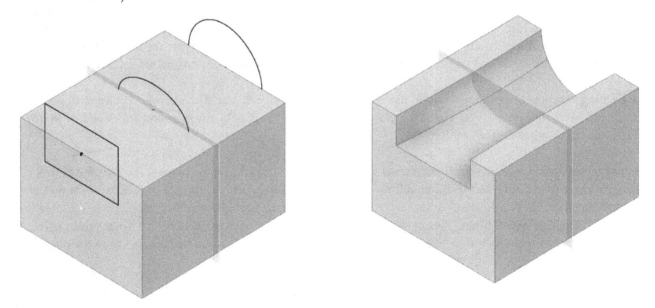

Examples
Example 1 (Millimetres)
In this example, you will create the part shown below.

Loft Features

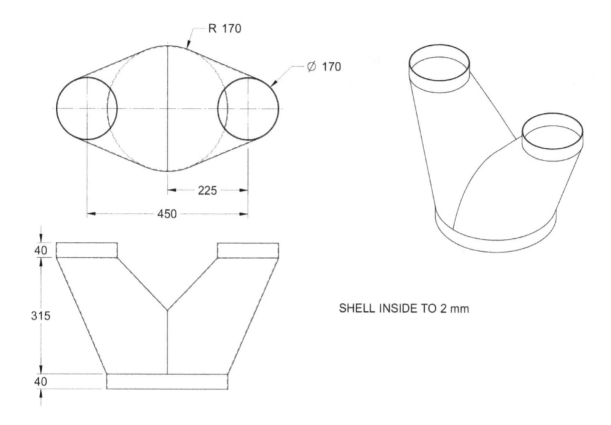

R 170

∅ 170

225

450

40

315

40

SHELL INSIDE TO 2 mm

1. Start **Autodesk Inventor**.
2. On the File Menu, click the **New** icon; the **Create New** File dialog appears. On this dialog, click **Templates > Metric**, and then click the **Standard (mm).ipt** template; a new part file is opened.
3. To start a new sketch, click **3D Model > Sketch > Create 2D Sketch** on the ribbon.
4. Select the XZ Plane and draw a circle of 340 mm diameter. Click **Finish Sketch** on the ribbon.
5. Create the *Extrude* feature with 40 mm thickness.

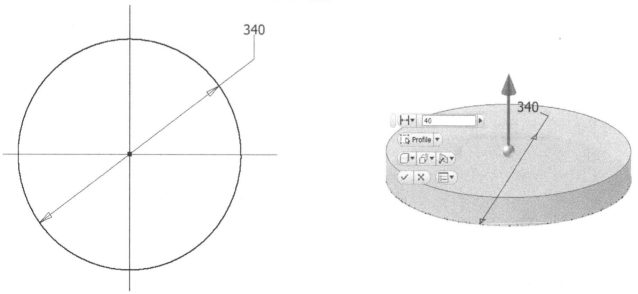

340

340

6. On the ribbon, click **3D Model > Work Features > Planes drop-down > Offset Plane** .

7. Click on the top face of the geometry. Type-in **315** mm in the **Offset** box and press Enter.
8. On the ribbon, click **3D Model > Sketch > Create 2D Sketch**, and then select the newly created plane.
9. Activate the **Circle Center Point** command and draw a circle of 170 mm diameter. Also, add dimensions and constraints to the circle, as shown. Click **Finish Sketch** on the ribbon.

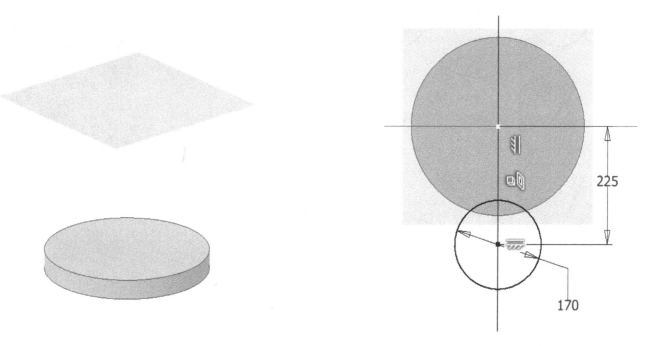

10. On the ribbon, click **3D Model > Create > Loft** .
11. Click on the circle and the top circular edge of the *Extrude* feature. Click **OK** to complete the *Loft* feature.

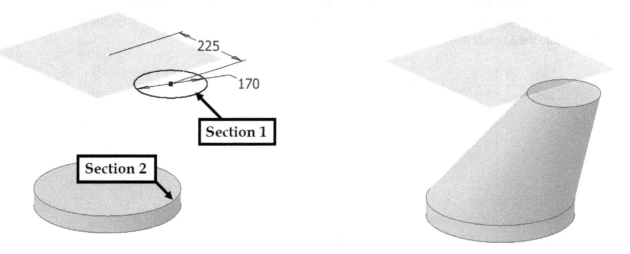

12. Activate the **Create 2D Sketch** command and click on the top face of the *Loft* feature.
13. On the ribbon, click **Sketch > Create > Project Geometry**, and click on the circular edge of the top face. Click **Finish Sketch** on the ribbon.
14. Activate the Extrude command and type **40** in the **Distance1** box. Press Enter.

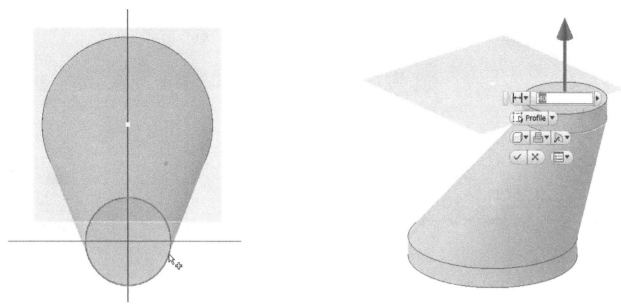

15. On the ribbon, click **3D Model > Pattern > Mirror**. Select the loft feature and the extruded feature on top of it.

16. Click the **Origin YZ Plane** icon on the Mirror dialog. Click **OK** to mirror the selected features.

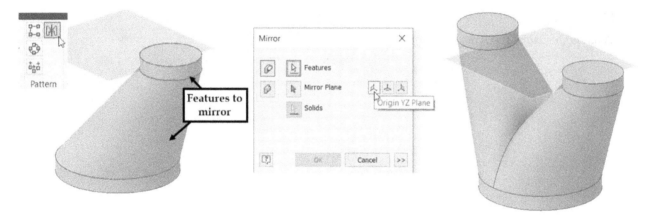

17. On the ribbon, click **3D Model > Modify > Shell** and click on the flat faces of the part geometry.

18. Type 2 in the Thickness box and press Enter. The part geometry is shelled.

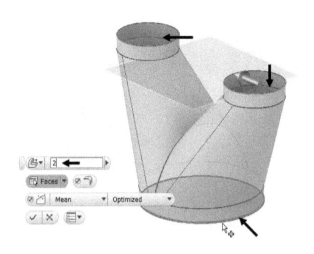

19. Save and close the part file.

Questions

1. Describe the procedure to create a *Loft* feature.

2. List any two options in the **Conditions** tab.

3. List the type of elements that can be selected to create a *Loft* feature.

4. What is the use of the **Area Loft** option?

Exercises
Exercise 1

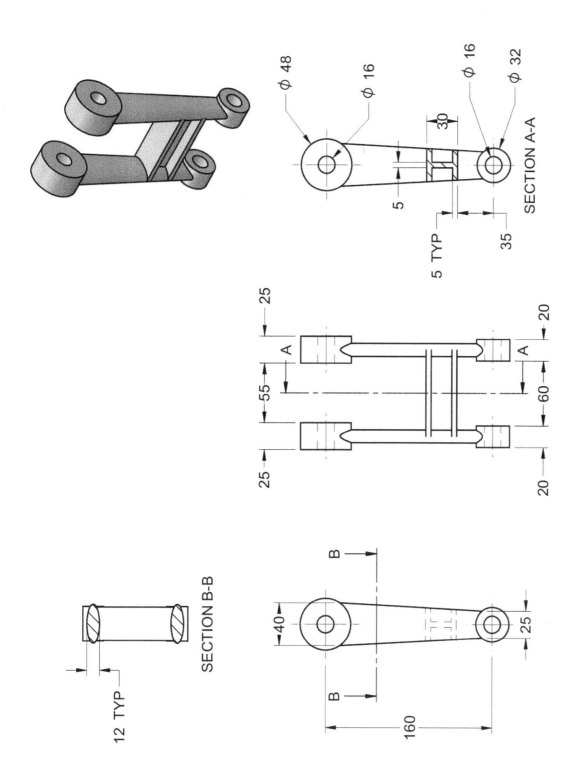

Chapter 8: Additional Features and Multibody Parts

Inventor offers you some additional commands and features which will help you to create complex models. These commands are explained in this chapter.

The topics covered in this chapter are:

- *Ribs*
- *Bend Part*
- *Multi-body parts*
- *Split bodies*
- *Combine bodies, and*
- *Emboss features*

Rib

This command creates rib features to add structural stability, strength and support to your designs. Just like any other sketch-based feature, a rib requires a two dimensional sketch. Create a sketch, as shown in figure and activate the **Rib** command (click **3D Model > Create > Rib** on the ribbon). Select the sketch; the preview of the geometry appears. You can add the rib material to either side of the sketch line or evenly to both sides. Click the **Symmetric** icon under the **Thickness** section to add material to both sides of the sketch line. Type-in the thickness value of the rib feature in the **Thickness** box. You can also set the depth of the rib, there are two options: **To Next** and **Finite**

. The **To Next** option terminates the rib on the next face and the **Finite** option creates the rib up to the specified distance. Note that you need to check the **Extend Profile** option while using the **Finite** option.

You can define the direction of the rib feature by using the **Normal to Sketch Plane** or **Parallel to Sketch Plane** option.

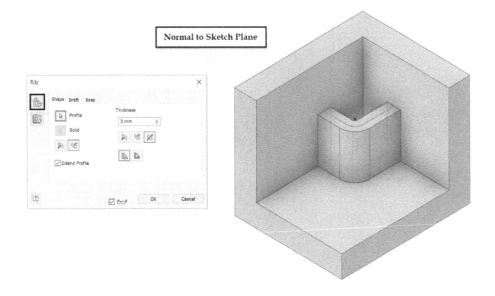

Normal to Sketch Plane

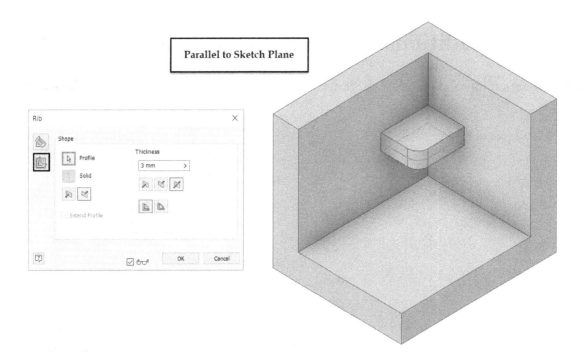

Applying Draft to the Rib Feature

Inventor allows you to apply draft to the rib features which is normal to sketch plane. To draft to the rib feature, click **Draft** tab and select **Hold Thickness > At Top.** Next, type-in a value in the **Angle** box; the draft is applied to the side faces of the rib feature. The thickness of the rib feature will remain the same at the top face.

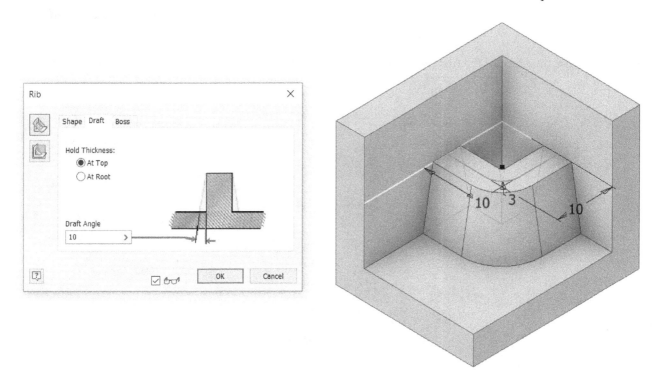

If you select **Hold Thickness > At Root**, the thickness of the rib feature will remain the same at the bottom.

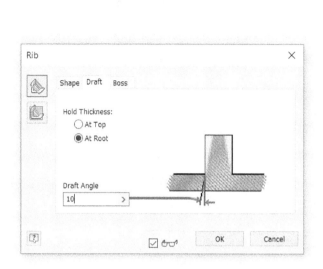

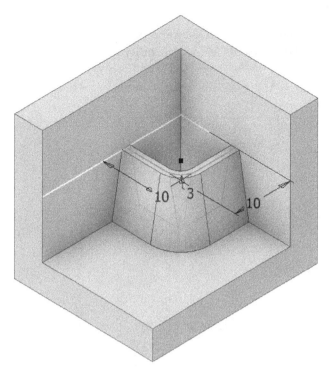

Adding a Boss to the Rib feature

Create a sketch for the rib feature and add a point to it. Make sure that the point is coincident with the sketch. Next, activate the **Rib** command and select the sketch; the preview of the rib feature appears along with the bosses. Click the **Boss** tab and notice that the **Select All** option is checked. As a result, all the points in the sketch are selected. If you want to select the points individually, then uncheck the **Select All** option, and click on the sketch points. After selecting the points, you need to specify the settings on the **Boss** tab. These settings are explained next.

Offset

This box is used to specify the height of the boss from the sketch plane of the rib feature.

Diameter

This box is used to specify the diameter of the boss feature.

Draft Angle

This box is used to add the draft to the boss feature.

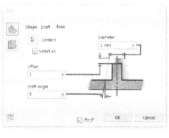

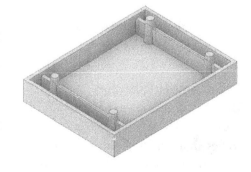

Bend Part

This command is used to bend a portion of the part geometry using a sketched line. Activate this command (on the ribbon, click **3D Model > Modify** panel **> Bend Part**) and click on the sketch line in the graphics window. Next, select the bend method from the drop-down available on the **Bend Part** dialog. There are three methods: **Radius + Angle**, **Radius + Arc Length** and **Arc Length + Angle**.

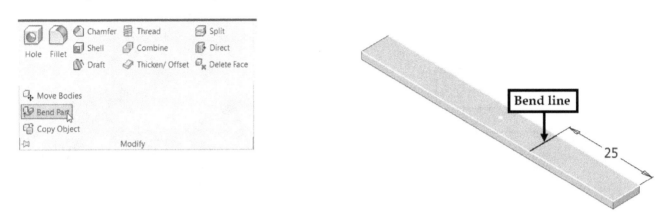

The **Radius + Angle** method creates a bend using the bend radius and angle values.

The **Radius + Arc Length** method creates a bend using the bend radius and arc length values.

The **Arc Length + Angle** method creates a bend using the arc length and bend angle values.

Next, specify the side of the part to be bend using the **Bend left** or **Bend right** or **Bend Both** icons. If you want to flip the direction, then click the **Flip bend direction** icon and click **OK**.

Multi-body Parts

Inventor allows the use of multiple bodies when designing parts. This opens the door to several design techniques that would otherwise not be possible. In this section, you will learn some of these techniques.

Creating Multibodies

The number of bodies in a part can change throughout the design process. Inventor makes it easy to create separate bodies inside a part geometry. Also, you can combine multiple bodies into a single body. In order to create multiple bodies in a part, first create a solid body, and then create any sketch-based feature such as extruded, revolved, swept, or loft feature. While creating the feature, ensure that the **New Solid** icon is selected on the dialog. Next, expand the **Solid Bodies** folder in the **Model** Window and notice the multiple solids.

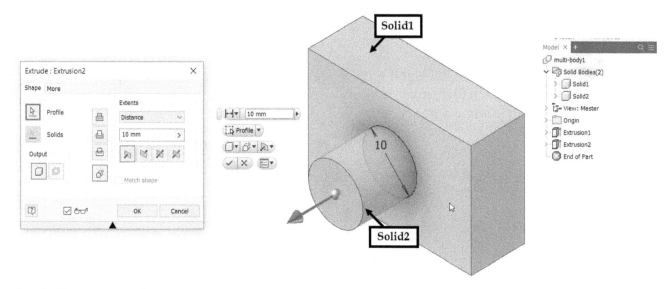

The Split command

The **Split** command can be used to separate single bodies into multiple bodies. This command can be used to perform local operations. For example, if you apply the shell feature to the front portion of the model shown in figure, the whole model will be shelled. To solve this problem, you must split the solid body into multiple bodies (In this case, separate the front portion of the model from the rest).

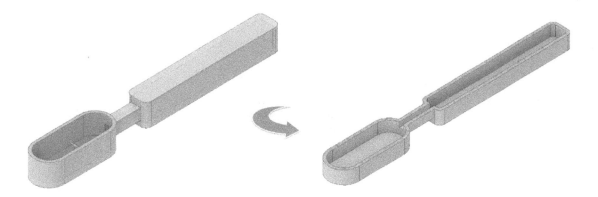

To split a body, you must have a splitting tool such as planes, sketch elements, surface, or bodies. In this case, a surface can be used as a splitting tool. To create a surface, click **3D Model > Surface > Ruled Surface** on the ribbon and click the **Normal** icon on the **Ruled Surface** dialog. Next, click on the edge of the split body. Specify the distance under the **Extend** section and click the **Flip** icon to reverse the direction. Click **OK** to create the ruled surface. You can use this ruled surface as a split tool to split the solid body.

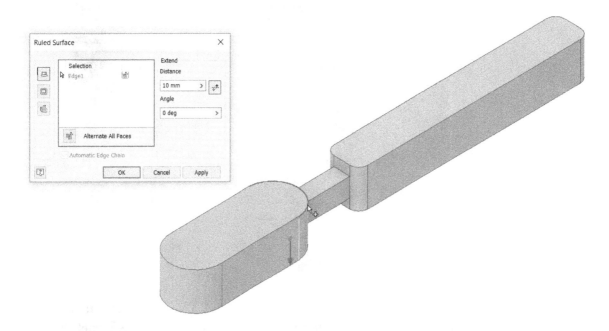

Activate the **Split** command (click **3D Model > Modify > Split** on the ribbon). On the **Split** dialog, click the **Split Solid** icon; the solid body gets selected automatically. Click the **Split Tool** selection button and select the ruled surface from the graphics window. Click **OK**; the solid body is split into two separate bodies.

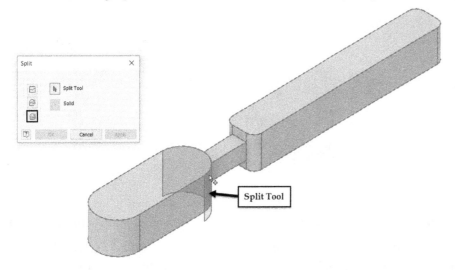

Now, create the shell feature on the split body.

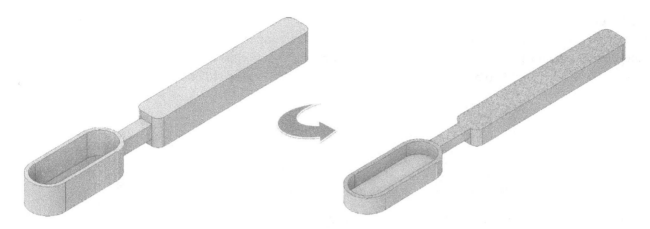

Join

If you apply fillets to the edges between two bodies, it will show a different result as shown in figure. In order to solve this problem, you must combine the two bodies.

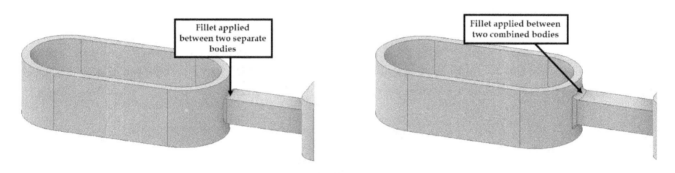

Activate the **Combine** command (on the ribbon, click **3D Model > Modify > Combine**) and click the **Join** icon on the **Combine** dialog. Next, select the two bodies. Click **OK** on the dialog to join the bodies. Now, apply fillets to the edges.

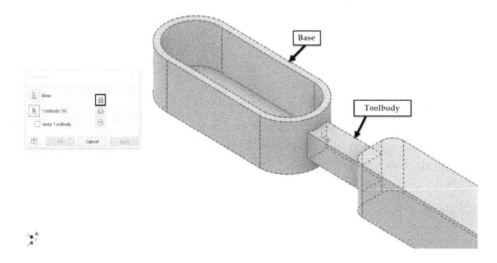

Intersect

By using the **Intersect** option, you can generate bodies defined by the intersecting volume of two bodies. Activate **Combine** command (click **3D Model > Modify > Combine** on the ribbon). On the **Combine** dialog, click the **Intersect** icon and select two bodies. Click **OK** to see the resultant single solid body.

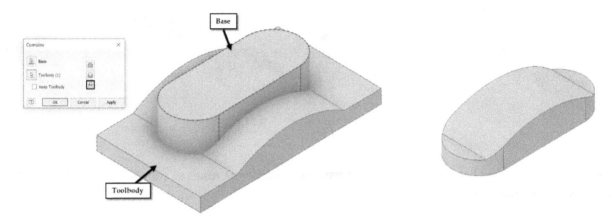

Cut

This option performs the function of subtracting one solid body from another. Activate the **Combine** command (click **3D Model > Modify > Combine** on the ribbon) and click the **Cut** icon on the **Combine** dialog. Next, select the base and tool body. Click **OK** to subtract the tool body from the base.

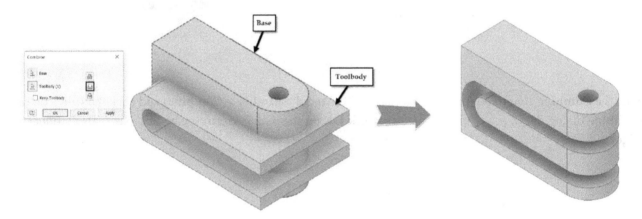

Emboss

This command embosses or engraves a text or shape on to the model geometry. For example, to engrave or emboss a sketch on to the cylindrical face of the model, first start a sketch on the plane, as shown. Next, click **Sketch > Create > Text** on the ribbon) and click in the graphics window. Type the text in the **Format Text** dialog, and then click **OK**. Next, apply the **Vertical** Constraint between the midpoint of the text frame and the sketch origin. Click **Finish Sketch** on the ribbon.

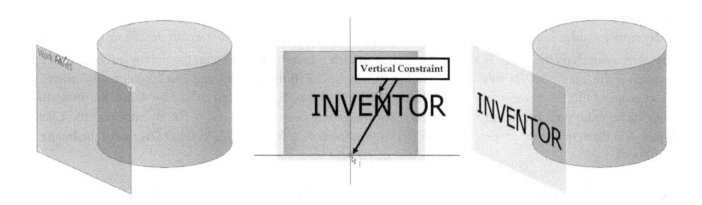

Activate the **Emboss** command (click **3D Model > Create > Emboss** on the ribbon) and click the **Emboss From Face** icon on the **Emboss** dialog. Click the **Profile** selection button and select the sketch. Next, type a value in the **Depth** box, and then click the **Top Face Appearance** swatch located below the **Depth** box. On the **Appearance** dialog, select **Steel Blue** from the drop-down and click **OK**. Check the **Wrap on Face** option and select the

cylindrical face. Click the **Direction 2** icon so that the arrow on the sketch points towards the model. Click **OK** to emboss the text. If you want to engrave the text, right click on the **Emboss** feature in the **Model** window, and select the **Edit Feature**. Next, click the **Engrave From Face** icon, specify the **Depth** value, and click **OK**.

The **Emboss/Engrave from Plane** option embosses or engraves the sketch based on the position of the sketch plane.

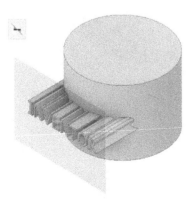

Decal

This command adds images to the model faces. For example, to add an image to the cylindrical face of a model, first start a sketch on the plane, as shown. Next, click **Sketch > Insert > Image** on the ribbon and browse to the location of the image file. The format of the image file can be GIF, Bitmap, JPEG, and PNG. You can also select an Excel or Word file. Select the image file and notice the **Link** option. This option if checked will link the image file with the Inventor part. If you leave it unchecked, the image will be embedded inside the Inventor part file. Click **Open**, and then click in the graphics window to position the sketch. Right click and select **OK** to exit the **Image** command.

To resize the image, click on the lower right corner point of the image, press and hold the left mouse button, and then drag. To move the image, press and hold the left mouse button on it, and then drag; the image is moved. Apply constraints between the image and model edges to perfectly position the image. Click **Finish Sketch** on the ribbon to complete the sketch.

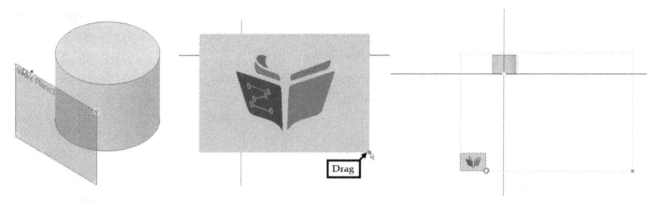

Activate the **Decal** command (on the ribbon, click **3D Model > Create > Decal**) and select the image. Next, click on the face to add the image, and then click **OK**.

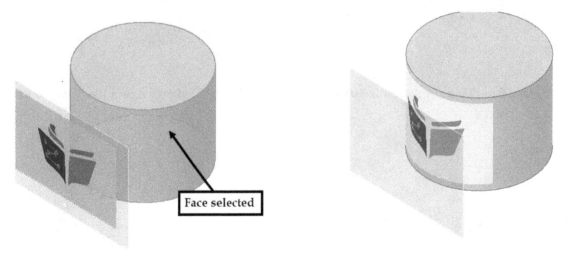

Examples

Example 1 (Inches)

In this example, you will create the part shown next.

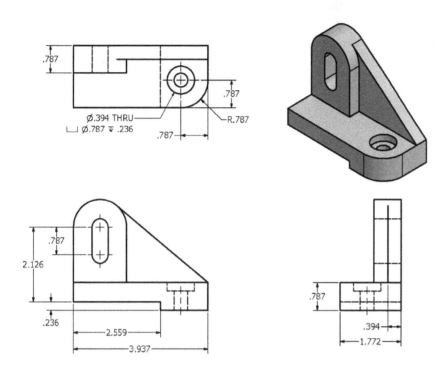

1. Start **Autodesk Inventor 2019.**
2. On the **Quick Access Toolbar**, click **New**; the **Create New File** dialog pops up.
3. On this dialog, click **Templates > en-US**. Select the **Standard.ipt** template and click **Create**.
4. On the ribbon, click **3D Model > Sketch > Create 2D Sketch** and draw the sketch on the XZ plane, as shown below. Next, click **Finish Sketch** on the ribbon.
5. On the ribbon, click **3D Model > Create > Extrude**. On the **Extrude** dialog, select **Extents > Distance** and enter 0.787 in the **Distance1** box. Click the **Direction1** icon and click **OK** to create the *Extrude* feature.

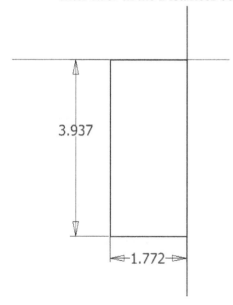

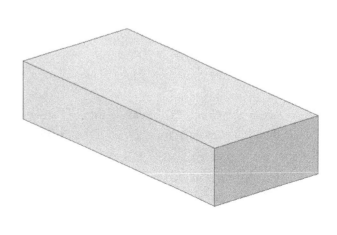

6. Activate the **Create 2D Sketch** command and click on the **XY** plane in the **Model** window by expanding the **Origin** folder.
7. Draw the sketch and add dimensions to it, as shown. Click **Finish Sketch** on the ribbon.
8. Activate the **Extrude** command and select the sketch. On the **Extrude** dialog, select **Extents > Distance** and enter 0.787 in the **Distance1** box. Click **OK** to complete the Extrude feature.

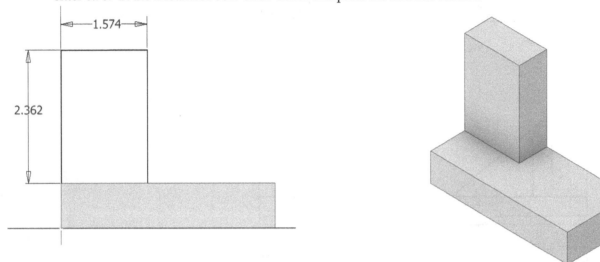

9. On the ribbon, click **3D Model > Modify > Fillet**, and then click **Full Round Fillet** on the **Fillet** dialog.
10. Select the faces of the second feature in the sequence, as shown. Click **OK** to create the full round fillet.

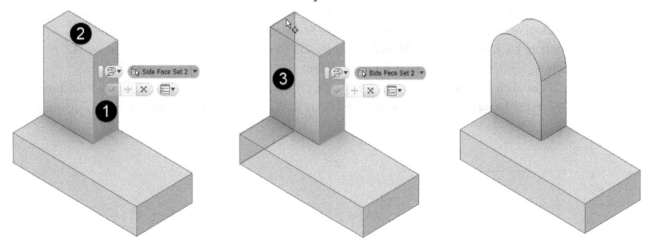

11. Activate the **Create 2D Sketch** command and click on the **XY** plane in the **Model** window. Draw an inclined line, as shown.
12. On the ribbon, click **Sketch > Constrain > Tangent**, and then select the inclined line and the curved edge; the line is made tangent to the edge.
13. On the ribbon, click **Sketch > Constrain > Coincident Constraint**, and then select the endpoint of the inclined line and the curved edge; the endpoint of the line is made coincident to the edge.
14. Likewise, make the other endpoint of the line coincident with the vertex point, as shown. Click **Finish Sketch** on the ribbon.

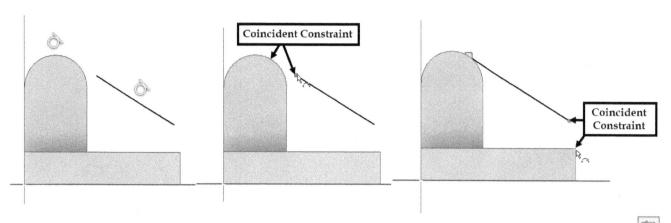

15. Click **3D Model > Create > Rib**, on the ribbon. On the **Rib** dialog, click the **Parallel to Sketch Plane** icon.

16. Click the **Profile** button and select the sketch (if not already selected). Click the **Direction 1** icon.

17. Type-in **0.394** in the **Thickness** box and click the **To Next** icon. Next, click the **Direction 1** icon in the **Thickness** area. Click **OK** to create the *Rib* feature.

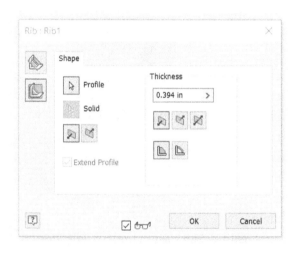

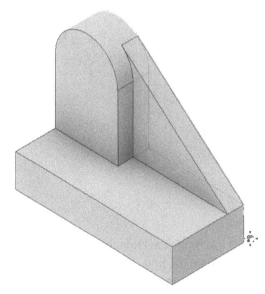

18. Activate the **Create 2D Sketch** command and click on the front face of the second feature, as shown.
19. On the ribbon, click **Sketch > Create > Rectangle** drop-down **> Slot Center to Center**.
20. Draw a slot and add dimensions to it, as shown. Click **Finish Sketch** on the ribbon.

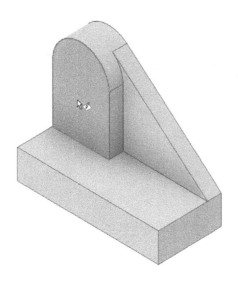
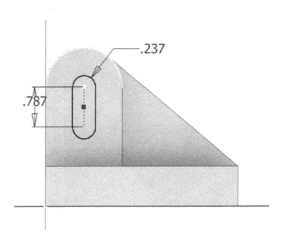

21. Activate the **Extrude** command and select the sketch. On the **Extrude** dialog, click the **Cut** icon and select **Extents > All**. Next, click **OK** to create the *Cutout* feature.
22. Add a fillet of 0.787 in radius to the right vertical edge of the rectangular base.

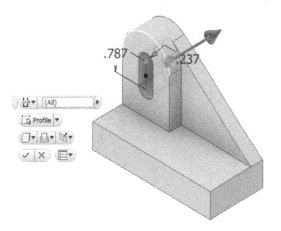
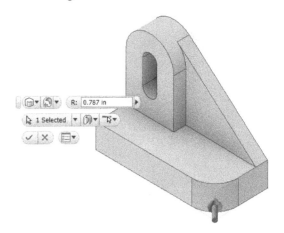

23. Activate the **Hole** command and click on the top face of the first feature. Next, select the curved edge of the fillet; the hole is made concentric to the fillet.
24. On the **Properties** panel, specify the settings, as shown. Next, click **OK** to create the hole.

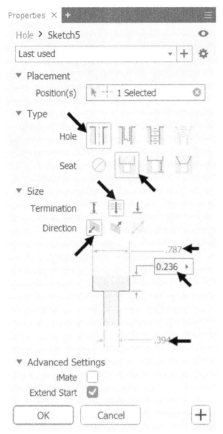

25. Activate the **Create 2D Sketch** command and select the front face of the rectangular base.
26. Draw a sketch and add dimensions to it. Click **Finish Sketch** on the ribbon.
27. Create an *Extruded Cutout* feature using the sketch.

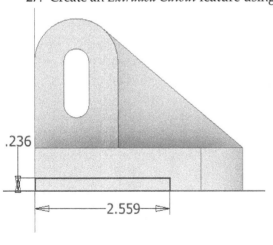

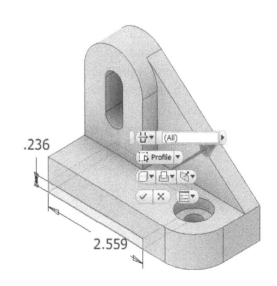

28. Save and close the part file.

Example 1 (Millimetres)

In this example, you will create the part shown next.

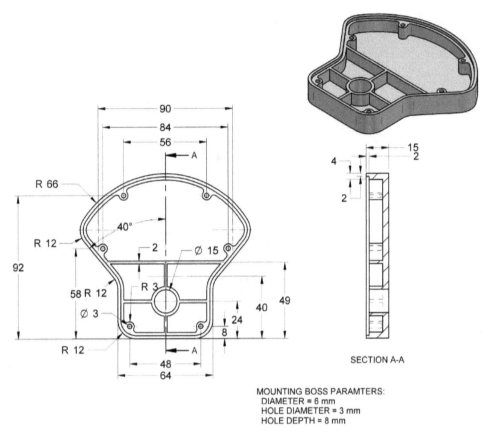

SECTION A-A

MOUNTING BOSS PARAMTERS:
DIAMETER = 6 mm
HOLE DIAMETER = 3 mm
HOLE DEPTH = 8 mm

FILLET MOUNTING BOSS CORNER 2 mm

1. Start **Autodesk Inventor 2019**.
2. On the File Menu, click the **New** icon; the **Create New File** dialog appears. On this dialog, click **Templates > Metric**, and then double-click on the **Standard (mm).ipt** template; a new part file is opened.
3. To start a new sketch, click **3D Model > Sketch > Create 2D Sketch** on the ribbon, and then select the XZ Plane.
4. On the ribbon, click **Sketch > Create > Line** and draw the sketch, as shown in figure below. Also, create a horizontal centerline passing through the origin.
5. On the ribbon, click **Sketch > Pattern > Mirror**, and then mirror the horizontal and inclined line about the centerline. Next, apply the **Coincident Constraint** between the endpoints, as shown.

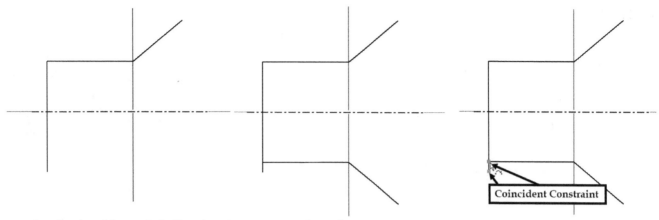

6. On the ribbon, click **Sketch > Create > Arc drop-down > Arc Three Point**, and then create an arc by specifying the points in the sequence, as shown.

7. Apply dimensions to the sketch. Also, apply the **Coincident Constraint** between the center point of the arc and the sketch origin.

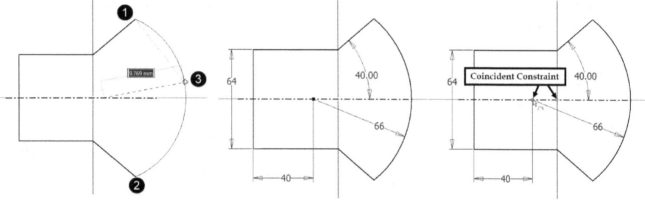

8. On the ribbon, click **Sketch > Create > Fillet drop-down > Fillet**, and then type **12** in the **Fillet** dialog. Create the fillet at the sharp corners, as shown.

9. On the ribbon, click **Sketch > Constrain > Dimension**. Add a linear dimension between the centerpoints of the fillets, as shown.

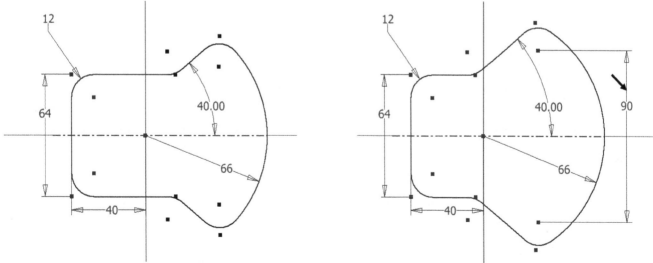

10. Click **Finish Sketch** on the ribbon, and then create the *Extrude* feature of 15 mm depth.

11. Create the *Shell* feature of 4 mm depth.

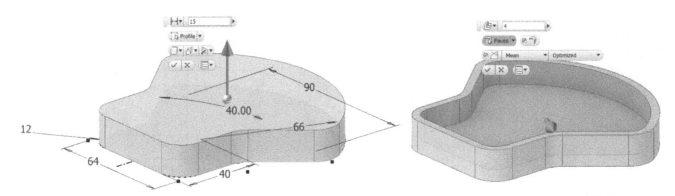

12. On the ribbon, click **3D Model > Plastic Part > Lip** . On the **Lip** dialog, click the **Groove** icon.
13. Click on the inner edge of the *Shell* feature to specify the path edges. Next, click the **Guide Face** icon and select the top face of the model.
14. Click the **Groove** tab on the **Lip** dialog and sect the **Height** and **Width** values to 2. Click **OK** to create the groove feature.

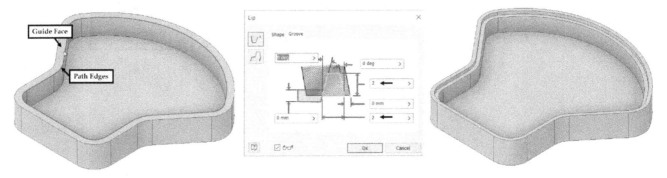

15. On the ribbon, click **3D Model > Sketch > Create 2D Sketch**, and then click on the top face of the groove feature.
16. Create sketch points and add dimensions to them. Click **Finish Sketch** on ribbon.

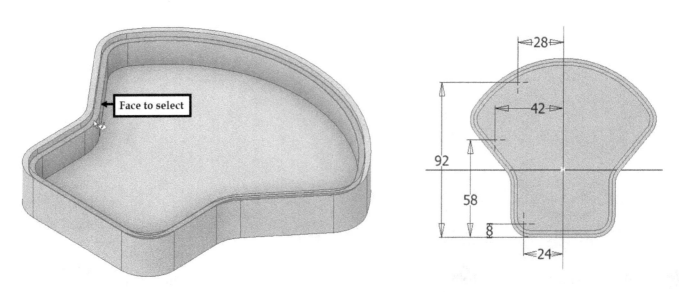

17. On the ribbon, click **3D Model > Plastic Parts > Boss** . On the **Boss** dialog, click the **Thread** icon. Next, select **Placement > From Sketch**; the points are selected and the preview of the bosses is displayed.

18. Click the **Thread** tab on the **Boss** dialog. Next, set the **Thread diameter** to 6.

19. Check the **Hole** option, and then select **Depth** from the drop-down displayed under it. Next, set the **Thread Hole diameter** to 3. Enter 8 in the **Thread Hole depth** box.

20. Enter 1 in the **Inner Draft Angle** and **Outer Draft Angle** boxes, and click **OK** to close the dialog.

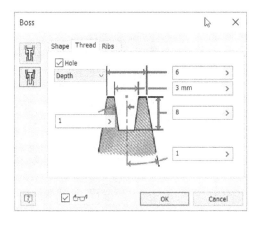
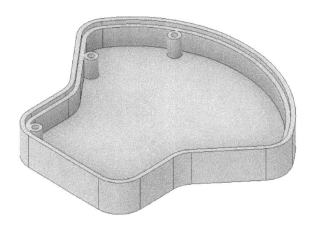

21. On the ribbon, click **3D Model > Pattern > Mirror** and select the **Boss** feature from the **Model** window.

22. On the **Mirror** dialog, click the **Origin YZ Plane** icon. Click **OK** to mirror the bosses.

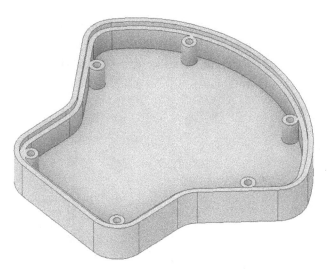

23. On the ribbon, click **3D Model > Modify > Fillet** and select the edges where the mounting bosses meet the walls of the geometry.

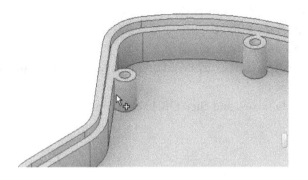 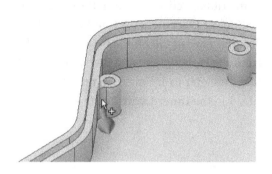

24. Type **2** in the **Radius** box on the Mini toolbar. Click the **OK** button to fillet the selected edges.

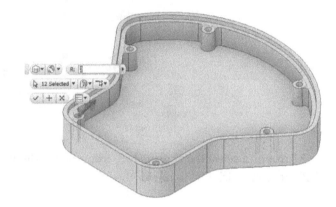

25. On the ribbon, click **3D Model > Sketch > Create 2D Sketch** and select the top face of the groove.
26. Create a sketch using the **Line** command and add dimensions to it.
27. On the ribbon, click **Sketch > Create >Point** and select the intersection point between the vertical and horizontal lines, as shown. Click **Finish Sketch** on the ribbon.

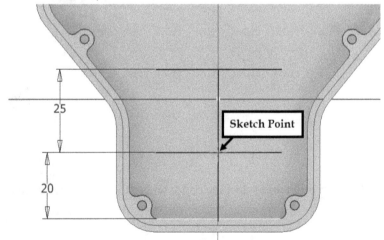

28. On the ribbon, click **3D Model > Create > Rib** and select the horizontal lines of the sketch.

29. On the **Rib** dialog, type **1** in the **Thickness** box and click the **Symmetric** icon.

30. Click the Boss tab and enter **17** in the **Diameter** box. Next, enter **0** in the **Offset** and **Draft Angle** boxes. Click **OK** to create the rib feature along with a boss.

31. In the **Model** window, expand the **Rib** feature and right click on the Sketch. Next, select **Visibility** from the shortcut menu; the sketch used for the rib feature is visible.

32. Activate the **Rib** command and select the vertical line of the sketch. Enter 1 in the **Thickness** box, and then uncheck the **Extend Profile** option. Click **OK** to complete the rib feature.

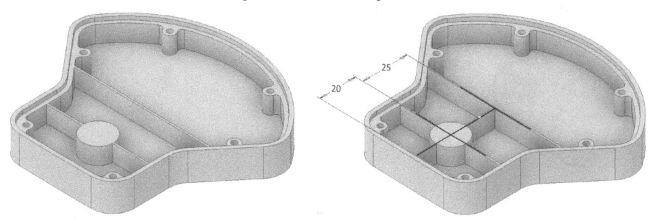

33. Activate the **Hole** command and notice that the sketch point is selected, automatically.

34. On the **Properties** panel, set the **Hole** type to **Simple Hole** and **Seat** type to **None**. Next, type **15** in the **Hole diameter** box and click **OK**.

35. In the **Model** window, expand the **Rib** feature, right-click on the sketch, and then deselect the **Visibility** option.

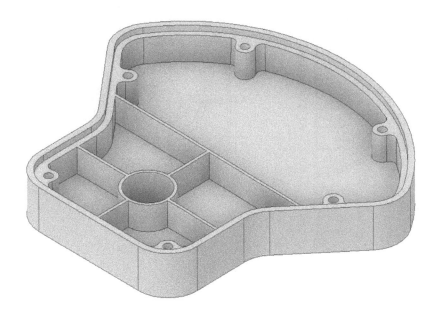

36. Save and close the file.

Questions

1. How to add a boss to a rib feature?

2. How many types ribs of can be created in Inventor?

3. Why do we create multi body parts?

4. What are the three emboss types available on the **Emboss** dialog?

Exercises
Exercise 1 (Millimeters)

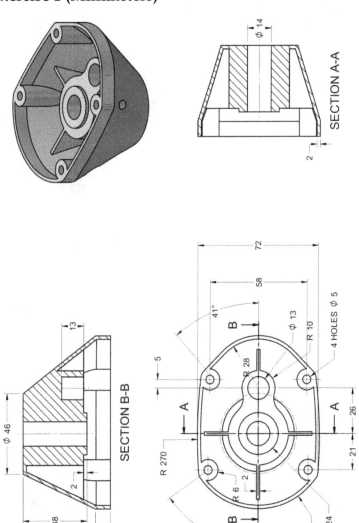

Exercise 2 (Millimeters)

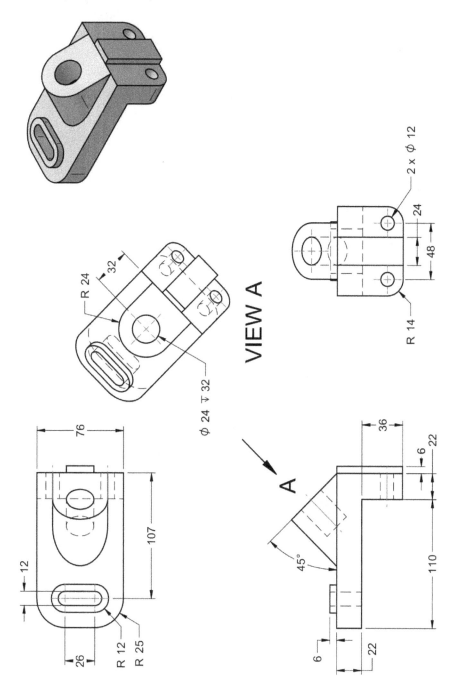

R 24
32
Ø 24 ⊽ 32

VIEW A

2 x Ø 12
24
48
R 14

76
107
12
26
R 12
R 25

36
6
22
110
45°
6
22

A

Exercise 3 (Inches)

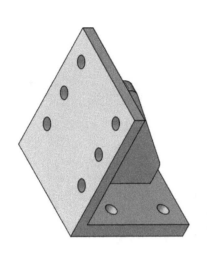

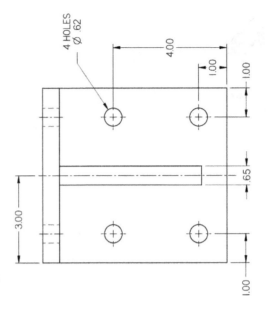

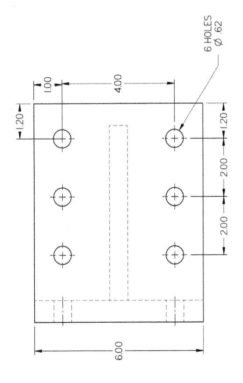

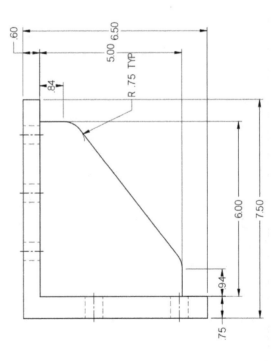

Chapter 9: Modifying Parts

In design process, it is not required to achieve the final model in the first attempt. There is always a need to modify the existing parts to get the desired part geometry. In this chapter, you will learn various commands and techniques to make changes to a part.

The topics covered in this chapter are:

- *Edit Sketches*
- *Edit Features*
- *Suppress Features*

Edit Sketches

Sketches form the base of a 3D geometry. They control the size and shape of the geometry. If you want to modify the 3D geometry, most of the times, you are required to edit sketches. To do this, click on the feature and select **Edit Sketch**. Now, modify the sketch and click **Finish Sketch** on the ribbon. You will notice that the part geometry updates immediately.

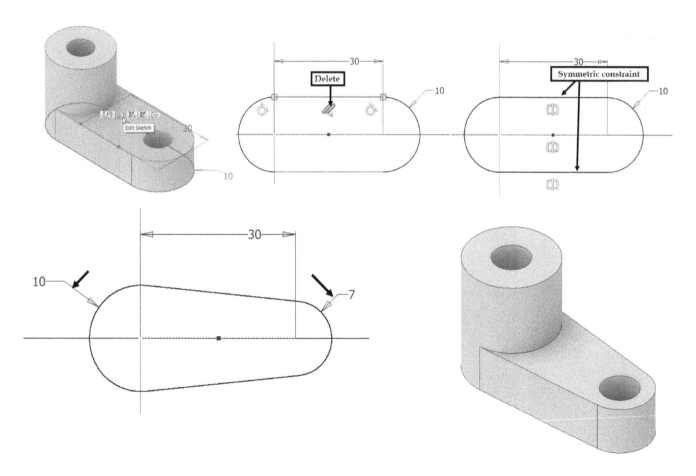

Edit Feature

Features are the building blocks of a model geometry. To modify a feature, click the right mouse button on it and select **Edit Feature**. The dialog related to the feature appears. On this dialog, modify the parameters of the feature and click **OK**. The changes take place immediately.

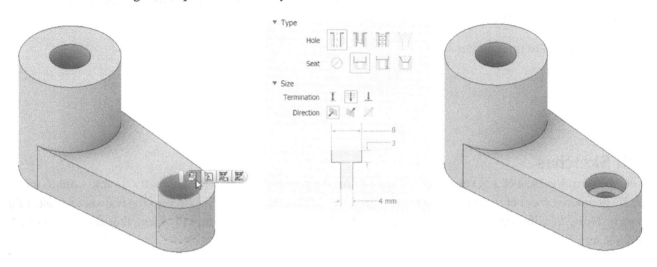

Suppress Features

Sometimes you may need to suppress some features of a model geometry. In the Model window, right-click on the feature to suppress, and then select **Suppress Features**.

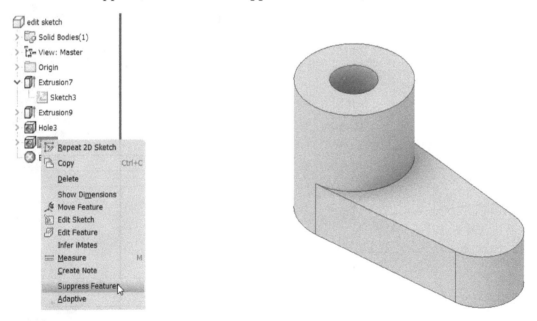

Resume Suppressed Features

If you want to resume the suppressed features, then right click on the suppressed feature in the Model window and select **Unsuppress Features**; the feature is resumed.

Modifying Parts

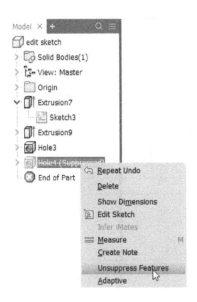

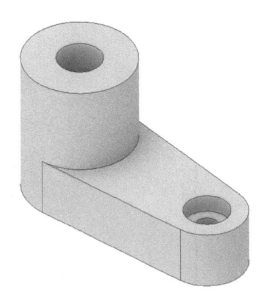

Examples

Example 1 (Inches)

In this example, you will create the part shown below, and then modify it.

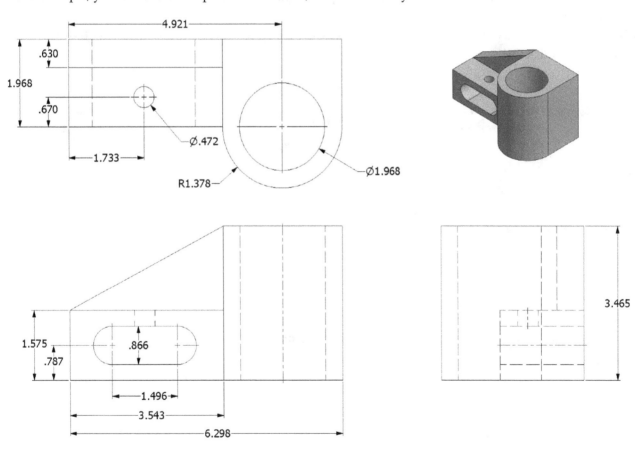

1. Start **Autodesk Inventor 2019** and open a part file and create the part using the tools and commands available in Inventor.

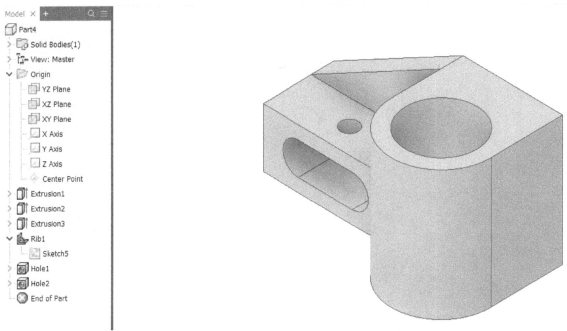

2. Click on the large hole and select **Edit Hole**; the **Properties** panel appears. On the **Properties** panel, select **Seat > Counterbore**.

3. Enter **1.378**, **1.968**, and **0.787** in the **Diameter**, **Counterbore Diameter**, and **Counterbore Depth** boxes, respectively. Click **OK**.

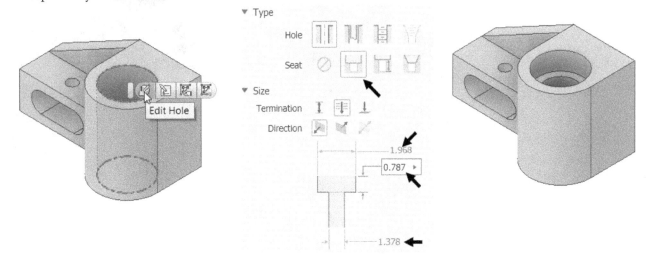

4. Click on the rectangular *Extrude* feature and select **Edit Sketch**. Modify the sketch, as shown. Click **Finish Sketch**.

Modifying Parts

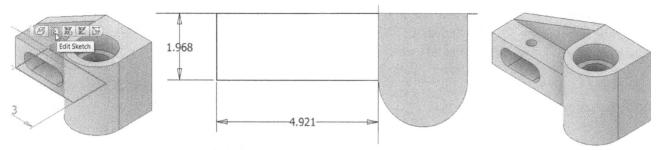

5. Click on the slot and select **Edit Sketch**.

6. Delete the length dimension of the slot, and then add a new dimension between the right-side arc and right vertical edge.

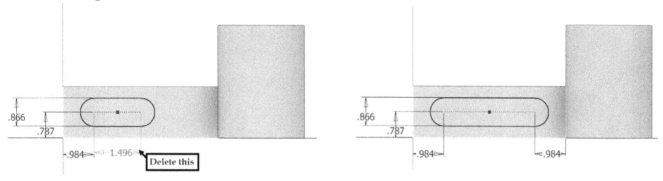

7. Delete the dimension between the center line of the slot and the horizontal edge.

8. Apply the **Horizontal** constraint between the centerpoint of the slot and the midpoint of the left vertical edge. Click **Finish Sketch** on the ribbon.

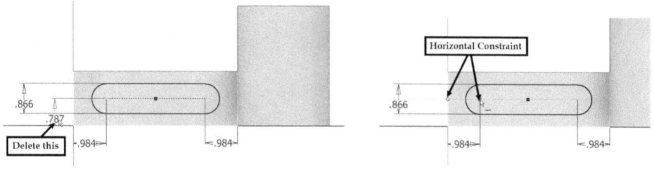

9. Click on the small hole, and then click **Edit sketch**. Next, delete the positioning dimensions.

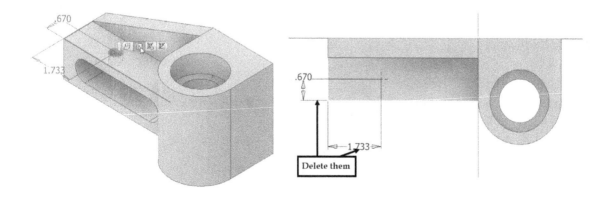

10. Create a construction line and make its ends coincident with the corners, as shown below.
11. On the ribbon, click **Sketch > Constrain > Coincident** and select the hole point. Next, select the midpoint of the construction line. Click **Finish Sketch** on the ribbon.

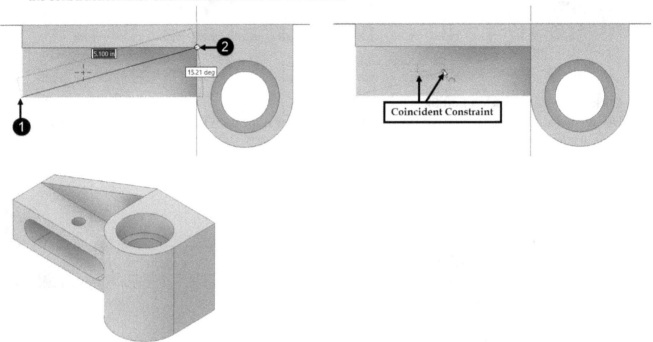

12. Now, change the size of the rectangular extrude feature. You will notice that the slot and hole are adjusted automatically.

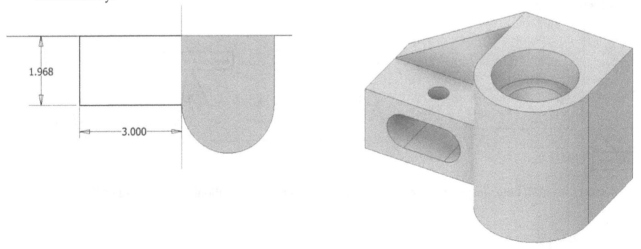

13. Save and close the file.

Example 2 (Millimetres)
In this example, you will create the part shown below, and then modify it using the editing tools.

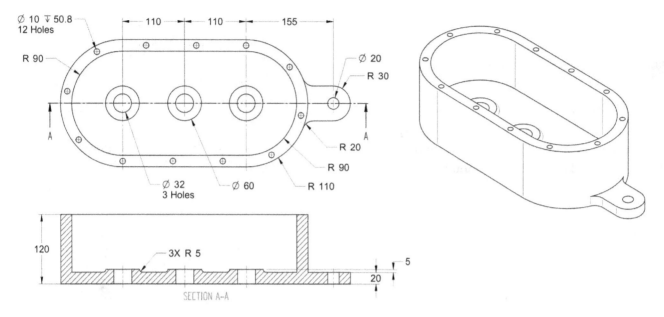

1. Start **Autodesk Inventor 2019**.
2. Click the **File** menu button located at the top left corner. On the **File** menu, click **New.** On the **Create New File** dialog, click **Templates > Metric**, and then double-click on the **Standard (mm).ipt** template; a new part file is opened.
3. Create the part using the tools and commands in Inventor.
4. Click on the 20 mm diameter hole, and then click **Edit Hole**; the **Properties** panel appears.
5. On the **Properties** panel, select **Seat > Counterbore**.
6. Set the **Counterbore Diameter** to 30 and **Counterbore Depth** to 10. Click **OK** to close the panel.

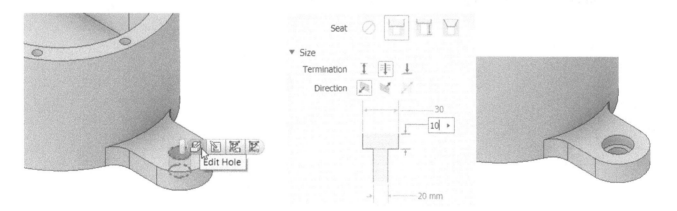

7. On the ribbon, click **3D Model > Modify > Direct** ⬚ , and then click **Move** on the Mini toolbar.
8. Click on the counterbore hole and the cylindrical face concentric to it. Next, select the arrow pointing toward right.
9. Press and hold the left mouse button on the selected arrow, drag, and then release it.
10. Type **20** in the value box that appears in the graphics window, and press Enter.

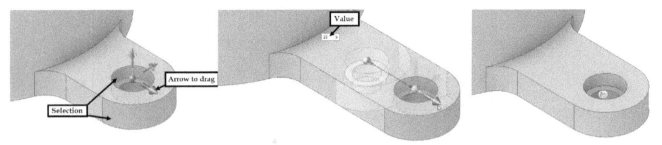

11. Click on anyone of the holes of the curve driven pattern, and then select **Edit Rectangular Pattern**.
12. Type 14 in the **Occurrence Count** box and click **OK** to update the pattern.

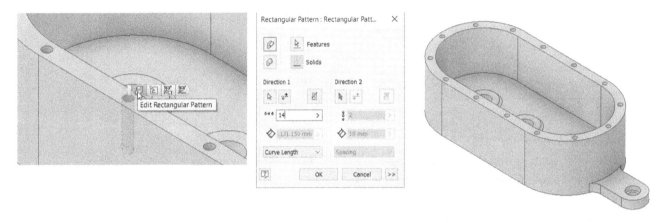

13. On the ribbon, click **3D Model > Modify > Direct**, and then select all the holes of the curve driven pattern.
14. Click on the top face of the geometry and select the **Move** option from the Mini toolbar.
15. Click on the arrow pointing upwards. Press and hold the left mouse button, and drag the mouse pointer down. Type -40 in dimension box and press Enter to update the model.

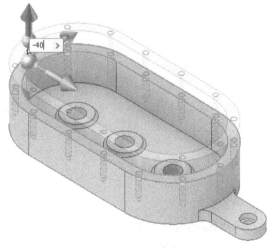

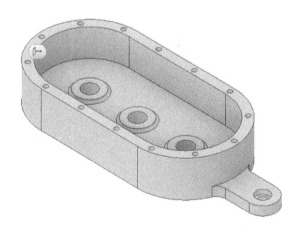

16. Save and close the file.

Questions

1. How to modify the sketch of a feature?
2. How to modify a feature directly?
3. How can you suppress a feature?

Exercises

Exercise 1

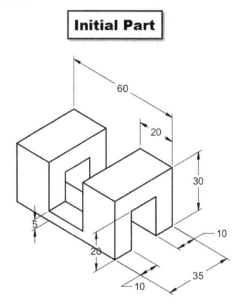

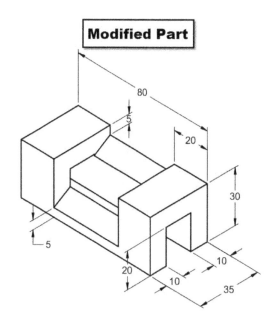

Index

All, 94
Angle to Plane around Edge, 86
Angular Dimensions, 41
Application Options, 24
Arc Tangent, 31
Arc Three Point, 31
Area Loft, 188
Assembly environment, 17
associativity, 14
Asymmetric, 92
At Root, 198
At Top, 198
Autodesk Inventor Help, 26
Automatic Dimensions and Constraints, 49
Bend Part, 200
Between, 93
Center Line Loft, 188
Center Point Arc, 32
Center Point Arc Slot, 37
Center Point Circle, 33
Center Point Slot, 36
Center to Center Slot, 35
Centerline, 50
Chamfer, 52, 129
Circular Pattern, 56, 151
Closed Loop, 187
Coil, 171
Coincident, 43
Collinear, 46
Color scheme, 25
Combine, 203
Concentric, 45
Constraint Settings, 48
Constraints, 43
Construction, 50
Control Vertex Spline, 58
Copy, 54
Corner Setback, 128
Counterbored Hole, 121
Countersink Hole, 122
Create New dialog, 23
Create new preset, 121
Creating Multibodies, 200
Customize, 21
Cut, 91, 204
Decal, 206
Dialogs, 21

Dimension, 39
Direction Condition, 184
Distance, 92
Distance and Angle chamfer, 130
Distance from Face, 94
Drawing environment, 18
Edit Feature, 224
Edit Sketches, 223
Ellipse, 39
Emboss, 204
Equal, 45
Extend, 53
Extend Start, 120
Extents, 92
Extrude Features, 81
Face Draft, 130
Face Fillet, 129
File Menu, 18
File Types, 16
Fillet, 51, 124
Fixed Plane, 131
Full Round Fillet, 129
Helical Cutout, 175
Hole, 117
Horizontal, 44
Inference, 48
Interpolation Spline, 59
Intersect, 91, 204
Inverted Fillet, 126
Join, 91, 203
Line, 30
Linear Dimensions, 40
Loft, 183
Loft Cutout, 190
Loft sections, 183
Look At, 97
Marking Menus, 23
Match Shape, 95
Midplane between Two Planes, 84
Midplane of Torus, 85
Mirror, 57, 146
Mirror Solids, 147
Model window, 19
Move, 54
Navigation wheel, 98
New Solid, 92
Normal to Axis through Point, 89

Normal to Curve at a Point, 89
Offset, 53
Offset from Plane, 83
Orbit, 97
Orientation, 167
Overall Slot, 35
Over-constrained Sketch, 42
Pan, 97
Parallel, 46
Parallel to Plane through Point, 84
Part environment, 17
Path & Guide Rail, 168
Path & Guide Surface, 169
Path sweeps, 164
Patterning the entire geometry, 151
Pitch and Height, 172
Pitch and Revolution, 173
Planes, 83
Polygon, 37
Profile scaling, 168
Project Geometry, 82
Quick Access Toolbar, 19
Rails, 186
Rectangle Two Point Center, 34
Rectangular Pattern, 57, 148
Resume Suppressed Features, 224
Revolution and Height, 172
Revolve, 82
Revolve Features, 82
Rib, 197
Rotate, 54
Ruled Surface, 201
Scale, 55
Search Help & Commands, 20
Shaded, 98
Shaded with Edges, 98
Sheet Metal environment, 18
Shell, 132
Shortcut Menus, 23
Show All Constraints, 49
Simple Hole, 118
Sketch Driven Pattern, 153
Smooth (G2) Condition, 186

Smooth G2 Fillet, 125
Spiral, 173
Split, 201
Start 2D Sketch, 29, 60
Status Bar, 20
Stretch, 55
Suppress, 151
Suppress Features, 224
Sweep, 163
Swept Cutout, 170
Symmetric, 47
Tangent, 46
Tangent Circle, 33
Tangent Condition, 185
Tangent to Surface through Edge, 87
Taper, 95, 167
Taper Tapped Hole, 123
Tapped Hole, 122
Thread, 123
Three Point Arc, 36
Three Point Center Rectangle, 34
Three Point Rectangle, 34
Three Points, 86
To, 93
To Next, 92
Trim, 53
Twist, 167
Two Coplanar Edges, 86
Two Distances chamfer, 130
Two Point Rectangle, 33
UCS, 90
User Interface, 16
Variable Radius Fillet, 127
Vertical, 44
View Cube, 21
Wireframe, 98
Wireframe with hidden edges, 99
Wireframe with Visible edges only, 99
Zoom, 97
Zoom All, 97
Zoom Selected, 98
Zoom window, 97

www.ingramcontent.com/pod-product-compliance
Lightning Source LLC
Chambersburg PA
CBHW080522060326
40690CB00022B/5001